The Trouble Is the Banks

The Trouble Is
the Banks

Letters to Wall Street

Edited by Mark Greif, Dayna Tortorici, Kathleen French,
Emma Janaskie, and Nick Werle

n+1 RESEARCH BRANCH SMALL BOOKS SERIES #4

n+1 Foundation
NEW YORK

Published 2012 by n+1 Foundation

68 Jay Street, Ste. 405

Brooklyn, New York

www.nplusonemag.com

Printed by the Sheridan Press

Manufactured in the United States of America

First Printing

Contents

Preface

A CERTAIN NUMBER OF THINGS ARE SACRED TO democracy. One of them is mail. You have to believe that a letter can reach its addressee, that no one will tamper with it, and that nobody is too fancy to receive a letter from anybody else. No one should be beyond a word of thanks, persuasion, or even censure, as long as it's honest and signed. The US Postal Service visits everyone's door without distinction. In the era of the internet, a democracy of email will have to develop, too.

Such is the premise of this book. *The Trouble is the Banks* collects letters that Americans (and one Canadian) wrote directly to executives and directors of five big US banks in fall 2011, at a time when protests were emerging in Occupy Wall Street camps across the country. Two presidential administrations had failed to bring our banks back under the restraint of law; the time had come to speak to bankers directly. The authors addressed their remarks to the highest employees of the banks where they were customers, or to executives whose names they had read in the news. Some letters were funny, others somber, but most were as polite as they were forceful. These writers spoke as citizens to citizens, trying to awaken the fortunate to their own consciences. The best of those letters are collected here.

Originally, this project was the brainchild of strangers who met in Zuccotti Park in New York City. They created a website called "Occupy the Boardroom" (OTBR). They devised a way for anyone with a computer to submit a letter to a named bank executive online, which would be delivered to that executive by email. OTBR also posted the letters in a long scroll, including messages without specific addressees, and invited site visitors to "check the mailbag," so that we could all read one another's thoughts.

Nearly 8,000 letters appeared in six weeks. The Americans who wrote in—to executives but also to each other—were not generally the ones visiting Occupy encampments. They were at home, fighting to keep their houses, working to pay their bills and debts. Many writers were older than the core that slept and assembled in camps and marched in the name of the 99%. They came from every state of the union. Their letters suggested that whatever their registered political party, they knew exactly why their fellow Americans were gathering outside in cities and towns, holding up signs until the police moved them on, and then coming back.

These writers rejected bank lobbying and funding of election campaigns. They deplored the harm done to the Constitution by the *Citizens United* decision. They asked why government had bailed out banks, but not citizens. They called for executives to pay tax rates at least equal to those of their employees. They advocated the restoration of Glass-Steagall and stronger banking laws, beyond Dodd-Frank, to prevent further risks to consumers. The people alone at home and the people in the parks knew the same things.

For many of us at OTBR and *n+1*, these letters name the reasons why we were in the parks and in the streets. They show that Americans are intelligent and honest, but also hopeful and optimistic. Their authors want to make a living in America, whether they were born here or came as immigrants. They know that we make our livings as allies, neighbors, and citizens, not by stealing the food out of others' mouths. Maybe most importantly, each and every letter focuses on the original source of trouble, the knot where a host of other powers intersect—from the government and civil society, to businesses small and big—and abuses and crimes radiate outward to cause epic destruction. The trouble is the banks. Too many mistakes and negligences of our era, and too many willful, selfish harms, have used finance as their shared instrument.

We don't think this book vilifies banking or bankers. Good people exist in the banks, too. That's what makes letters such as these valuable. They appeal to conscience, shared standards, and moral persuasion. If anyone knows the extent of the banks' wrongdoing it is those within the banks, who will also have to stand up and admit the full measures needed to stop it. With these bankers in mind, the letter writers argue against the irresponsibility in Wall Street's pleas of helplessness: *It's not me, it's the rules. It's my role. It's capitalism. If I weren't doing the wrong thing, somebody else would. The stockholders would have my head. The market will decide.* All the letters, because they come from citizens, represent equals speaking to equals. They name behaviors that shame the doers and harm the country. They say: Stop it. You're a human being. Banker, think for yourself. Become responsible. Wake up.

T HIS BOOK has taken nine months to edit, and it is the joint effort of two groups of volunteers. The original creators of Occupy the Boardroom built the site from scratch through amazing labor over just a few weeks. The team that prepared the letters for this printed format, made up of *n+1* volunteers and others who found a common purpose in Occupy, could move more deliberately. We first read all of the 8,000 letters posted in early fall, then chose what we felt were the best 200. We then reached out to all the authors we could locate to ask permission to reprint their letters. If the name of the author is printed here, we reached him or her and received permission. If the name and town information is missing, it means we could not find the author despite our best efforts. In these cases, we have tried to completely anonymize letters that originally were signed.

We added two appendices to the book. In Appendix A, we assembled mailing addresses so that you, the reader, can write letters to your compatriots in banking, too. In Appendix B, we tried to learn what our authors were talking about—what was going on at large that created their individual cases—by revisiting government investigations into banks' illegal practices and related settlements of the past four years, all of which we found in public records.

One final thing, though, is important to know about this book: it is not itself a document for a court of law. We have trusted the letter writers' ways of explaining their lives, and not rewritten or fact-checked their life stories independently. When asking permission, we made sure our authors attested that what they wrote was true as far as they knew and that their words were their own. We also used common sense and the record of public events in selecting them. This is the speech of the People, not any authority above them. We have enough sources speaking for the highly placed and visible. This is a book that gives the ideas, and feelings, of the rest of us.

—*Editors*

Letters

Overture

Didn't Get Loan Mod Due to Incorrect Phone Number on Application

TO: CHARLES H. NOSKI, BANK OF AMERICA

Hi Charles,

My name is Matt. You don't know me but I'm a Bank of America customer. A few years ago my Countrywide Mortgage was bought by Bank of America, and we've been together ever since. Currently, my home is underwater by about $150,000 and I've also been hit by hard times. I'm working two jobs to keep my home, but over the last two years I've tried (unsuccessfully) to do a loan modification. Three times I've tried to do that.

I won't go into all the details, but the last time I tried to get a loan mod I was turned down because I had put down my home phone number instead of my cell phone number. Since I'm never home, due to working sixty-five hours a week, I didn't get the messages that were left on my home phone answering machine. That's the reason I was denied a loan mod by Bank of America.

But every time I call and talk to someone I get a different story. I can talk to Rep. A for a few minutes, call back in thirty minutes and talk to Rep. B about the same issue and get a different answer. The left hand doesn't know what the right hand is doing. In the meantime, I'm slowly drowning in debt.

Then I found out that in 2009, Bank of America paid $0 in Federal Income Tax. It was pretty much the same for 2010 too, as I understand it. But you got almost $1 billion from taxpayers in the bailout. What did I get? Nothing. If I went out and tried to make money and didn't, why should the government pay me for my losses?

Does that make any sense to you, Charles? I don't understand how a company that doesn't carry its fair share by using legal loopholes created by your lapdogs (Worst Congress *Ever*!) to dodge paying its taxes is able to get a bailout. Yet I try to get a loan mod (because I love my home and want to stay in my home) like many other hardworking, honest, good American citizens, by earning money and paying taxes. The bailout helped you, it paid you and others at Bank of America bonuses and your *salary*—but I'm denied a break because I put down the wrong phone number on the application.

Perhaps someone there can explain this to me, because I just don't get it. I'd *really* appreciate it if someone would take a couple of minutes to explain this to me.

Sincerely,

Matt Seufert
Spring Valley, CA 91978

I Didn't Buy a House

I knew I couldn't afford a house, but I hoped that someday if I kept working hard, I'd be able to. Those zero-money-down, everybody-qualifies loan offers flooded my mailbox, but I didn't bite because I knew my income couldn't carry that much debt.

I've been a renter my whole life. Thanks to the actions of a greedy few, the economy has tanked and living the American Dream is farther out of reach for people like me than ever.

When people play by the rules but don't get rewards, and see others cheating and being rewarded despite the harm they cause, deep, seething anger is the result.

This social movement to hold financial institutions accountable for wrongdoing and to create a system of economic justice for all is just getting started.

We will create change because we're not just disaffected hippies. We're the disaffected middle class. And we're huge.

Like a large majority of the middle class, I don't have a ton of money in one of your banks, but I have a regular paycheck and savings that I cultivate consistently. Very soon, I'll be closing my accounts and moving to a credit union or a small community bank. I'll do everything I can, socially, politically, and economically, to help move the society I live in out of corporate domination and into a state of proper democracy where citizens can play by fair rules and reap earned rewards.

I'm willing to wait for my house. I'm willing to work for a better future not just for myself, but for future generations as well. There's a lot of people like me out there.

How many of you are there? What are you willing to work for?

Pamila Payne
Los Angeles, CA 90068

Too Much for a Sound Bite

People say the OWS protesters' demands are too vague. They're not. It's just that there are so many things to protest, it's difficult to lasso them into a sound bite or a sign. Anyone who has read a paper, listened to the radio, watched TV, tried to find a job, suffered through the recession, gotten seriously ill, tried to educate their children, retired, been sent to war, returned from war, lived on the Gulf Coast, and especially tried to get our corporate-owned Congress, President, and Supreme Court to listen to us, knows what those demands are. Anyone else is deaf, blind, greedy, uncaring, selfish, evil, or all of the above.

Kay Rosen
Gary, IN 46403

Goodbye

I've been a loyal Bank of America customer since 1982.

But I've just spent an afternoon with one of my husband's former students. She is a nurse, recently divorced. Her mortgage is with Bank of America. For eleven months, she has been desperately trying to refinance. She can't get anywhere with your loan department, except requests for forms she has already given you.

We did not bail you out to give executives more bloated salaries and bonuses. You got into a mess through reckless lending and we thought you would use the money to set those loans right, not cause more bankruptcies and more heartache.

I am going to close my Bank of America accounts and my two Bank of America Visas. Quietly. (In view of today's Citibank arrests—at 72 I have no desire to spend the night in jail.) I am going to take my money to a local credit union.

Please Don't Harass My Father Any Further....

TO: LLOYD H. DEAN, WELLS FARGO

Dear Lloyd,

In May 2007, I became the first person in my immediate family to get a degree, at age 38. I graduated owing more than $100,000 in private student loans. Payments were more than $1,100 per month. My 74-year-old retired father is the cosigner for most of these loans, but in September 2008, my dad lost $70,000 of his pension with the banks' collapse.

In December 2009, after just one year in the work-force, I was laid off due to cut-backs. For most of 2010, I wasn't able to find steady employment. In January 2011, I ran out of deferment with my private student loans. The banks began chasing my father as the cosigner. They have wrecked his line of credit and called in his home equity loan on which he never missed any payments.

In June 2011, my father saw a lawyer to try to get the payments reduced to something proportionate to his fixed income. In October 2011, he got word that the lawyer failed to get payments reduced enough. My dad wrote me a letter saying he had to sell his life insurance and rearrange his will to protect my sister and stepmom.

The letter arrived last Saturday.

He had a stroke on Sunday.

Now Wells Fargo is harassing him for payment of another student loan.

I am asking you to please suspend collection actions against my father until I have a job that will pay me enough to make the payments myself.

I always believed getting an education was the only way to succeed in life. Now I regret it every single day.

Sincerely,

Deena DeNaro
Durham, NC 27701

Foreclosures

A young couple purchased a new high-end home across the street for almost $600,000. They had only one income, from the husband who worked as a parochial high-school teacher. The wife was a stay-at-home mom. All the neighbors wondered how they could afford such a house. Answer: they couldn't. He did not lie on his application. Yet Chase granted him a mortgage with a monthly payment higher than his take-home salary. He was told he could refinance and magically get money from the home's appreciation. This, of course, led to foreclosure. More bank bungling of a legitimate offer, and ultimately a sale price of $285,000. This depressed the value of all nearby homes. And this gets repeated over and over, depressing our whole economy. Banks must be held accountable!

Darlene Stille
New Buffalo, MI 49117

Making Home Affordable?

TO: ELLEN V. FUTTER, JP MORGAN CHASE

I'm a carpenter, work has been very light since the crash, my wife works in a small factory earning $17 an hour, no insurance. We signed up for Making Home Affordable.* They reduced our mortgage by $400 a month. Why did we go though the process? We were not behind in our payments, we just had a hard time making ends meet. Nine months into the process they said we were not eligible, that they were going to start foreclosure if we could not come up with the $400 that we did not pay or we could refinance at a lower rate saving us from losing our house and in the process taking all the interest we had paid up to that point. . . Ten years, $120,000. I know that no one will read this letter but it makes me feel better. What makes you feel better, madame?

Michael G. Anderson
Vashon, WA 98070

* Announced in February 2009, the Making Home Affordable Program was a piece of the Obama administration's efforts to stabilize the housing and mortgage markets. It collaborated with lenders to develop standard guidelines to use when evaluating applicants for mortgage modifications.

My Furnace Guy

This week I had to call the gentleman who services my furnace. He is in his seventies, and it is hard for him to walk and even harder for him to climb up and down peoples' stairs. I asked him when he was going to retire. "Can't afford it!" he said. Forty years ago he bought into some kind of insurance deal and started paying $50. Not even pin money on Wall St., but he paid it every month for forty years, almost 500 months. At the end, because of systematic excessive risk and fraud in the financial system, he received from this investment the grand total of $5,000. He probably doesn't know much about the details of the Grand Casino that our financial system has become, but he knows enough to diagnose the problem: "They're all crooks." The rest of us are also figuring it out in growing numbers, and we are on our way. . . .

Joel Roache
Salisbury, MD 21801

I Have Noticed Since You Foreclosed on My House, You Sure Don't Take Care of It Like I Did

TO: JULIE M. WHITE, WELLS FARGO

Hi Julie,

I was just wondering why, after I owned my home for seven years and took care of it even while fighting to keep it after I was unfortunately laid-off from my company downsizing, you and Wells Fargo (Wachovia) have not given it the same love and appreciation I always did. You would think that for how aggressive you were to take it from me, you would have given it the same love and care that I always have.

Last time I drove by the lawn really needed cutting. The fence is looking really bad, and there are tree branches all over the roof. I was in the process of trying to pay some amount to show my commitment to keeping my home (which would mean I'd still be paying you), but your lawyer fees (something like $3,000 for being ninety days late) made my ability to pay you anything reasonable completely impossible.

Besides looking for work, I was volunteering on the board of an animal rescue trying to place animals that were displaced or left in backyards by other people who had lost their homes. I had to quit since I had nowhere to live myself. Because you cannot give me my house back, nor do I expect you to, I would hope you, Wells Fargo

(Wachovia), could at least donate to a non-profit animal rescue and help the animals that I no longer can. They have lost their homes too, not just those of us with the ability to write an email.

Hello John

Honestly, I don't really like what you've done with the place (America that is).

My Neighbor Tried to Work It Out with Bank of America, but Couldn't

TO: JOE L. PRICE, BANK OF AMERICA

My name's Hannah* and I live in Olympia, Washington. I lost my house last year. Kind of fair and square, really, because I had no way to pay the mortgage. I had run myself $120,000 in debt after having a brain injury and losing my ability to work. So I knew what was coming and had to prepare for it. My doctor told me to stop talking to the collections people because conversations with them were making me feel suicidal. He said that my best option was to focus on getting medically stable so that moving wouldn't kill me.

My neighbor Hannah* was also losing her house, and it made me curious because she was actually making

* Names have been changed.

money at the time. Maybe not enough money to pay the entire mortgage, but some. She had tried to negotiate with Bank of America, but they weren't able to deal with her and kept sending people out to threaten her. She started drinking a lot. At the time I had accepted my fate and I was feeling a lot calmer about it. So I talked to her to console her and help her through it. She finally did lose her house in December 2010. I did too.

Now the two houses from the two Hannahs sit empty. Mine was bought by a real estate investor. He is trying to fix it up to make it into a rental property, but it's taking more time than he anticipated. Hers is still for sale. That's right. B of A could have collected some portion of a mortgage from my neighbor, but didn't want to.

I don't understand the logic of your employer, Joe. You all had a chance to have my neighbor try to pay her mortgage, but you didn't take it. That seems weird. In my case, I was just some lady with brain damage and huge medical debt who might die, so I can see how the bank might want to get me out of the way so they could move forward and get a mortgage payment going as soon as they could. But you all really could have had a mortgage payment from my neighbor who had her mortgage with you.

I'm wondering, Joe, if you are seeing where all this foreclosure activity is getting us. For me, it has given me a somewhat macabre sense of humor. If your only priority over at B of A is your bottom line, such practices aren't panning out from a fiscal standpoint, and you might want to take a look at them.

225 Times as Much?
I Think It's Even Worse.

TO: BARBARA J. DESOER, BANK OF AMERICA

Dear Barbara,

I just got home from a twelve-hour day. I am exhausted. I am sure you can relate, as the jobs high up the corporate ladder require much more stamina than a regular office job.

But so does teaching.

I am an adjunct instructor at Pima Community College. I am held to ¾ time, so I'm not eligible for benefits like health care or state retirement. My paycheck for two weeks of trying to elevate Arizona college students from poverty—eighty-five of them in three separate courses—would probably not cover a dinner for two in your world.

Arizona's public schools are ranked forty-ninth out of the fifty states; we were forty-eighth until Alabama passed us a few years ago. Many of my students are unable to function in the new economy due to gaps in education. Many collect assistance and are eligible for food stamps.

Here's the thing, Barbara: so am I. I live below the poverty level despite the fact that few people can do what I do. I fear that as a society, we no longer view education as a priority at all. My friends who are bartenders pick up the tab for me, and very few adjuncts have any sort of representation within their institution. We are labor ghosts.

The Trouble is the Banks

Many colleges and universities rely increasingly on adjunct labor. Whereas all of my college and graduate school mentors were able to find permanent, full-time positions when they received their Masters of Fine Arts degrees in Creative Writing in the '70s and '80s, most of the teaching writers I know who are under 40 find themselves bent over this very barrel.

I work extremely hard, Barbara. I stay up late every night and often must set an alarm for 5 AM to finish prepping, grading, and designing materials. Many of my students need extra help, so I voluntarily meet them regularly in the college cafeteria. You can't be surprised that I have no office, given the extreme blow delivered to education funding after the enormous bank bailouts.

I love my students, so I am careful not to be bitter or detached simply because all of the permanent, full-time job tracks are being eliminated. People my age have simply come to expect much less in terms of job stability and compensation; we internalize the dynamic of job scarcity in ways that make us feel like failures. I cannot come close to earning what either of my parents make, and fear that I will be in dire need once I am too old to work.

I was in Lithuania for a seminar this summer. There are really great things for Lithuanians about the end of communist rule; to a large extent, they have reclaimed their culture and their freedom. But because of European Union economic developments and a lack of infrastructure for productive labor, as well as the end of the safety net that was the silver lining of USSR occupation, I saw old people eat out of garbage cans. Every day of my three-week stay, I would see the elderly and frail dumpster diving.

I am afraid that is my future.

So when I read today in the *Daily Kos* that the average bank executive makes 225 times what the average teacher makes, and because I am at the lower end of the teacher wage spectrum, I ask you, Barbara: How many of me do you really think you are worth to the world? 300 Maggies? 500? A thousand Maggies?

I am through internalizing such oppressive ideology. I am not talking about revolution, but about some accountability, less risk in speculation, and the end to the breaking down of vital infrastructure like community colleges, roads, dams, public safety, public transportation and everything else we all need to live in the name of preventing millionaires from feeling a little pinch every April.

Perhaps I am more important than you think. Not just me, but all people who devote their time to helping people learn, to keeping them safe and healthy.

Perhaps I am too big to fail.

Sincerely,

Maggie Golston
Tucson, AZ 85701

Innovative!

Sorry to be so late in writing! Just wanted to give you a pat on the back for collecting over $4,000 from a friend of mine on a Chase credit card with a $500 limit (on which she charged a little bit less than $500 worth of merchandise). It was a great example of the innovation in your industry!

How the American Dream Turned $60,000 Cash into $30,000 Debt

Hi,

I just wanted to pass along my story of how I bought into the myth of the American Dream, and it blew up in my face.

My wife and I were expecting our first child in 2005, and we thought we needed to settle down and find a safe, secure place for our growing family. We bought into a housing market that was climbing at unprecedented rates. Prices were incredibly high, and we knew what we could realistically afford. We put $35,000 cash down. We locked in a low, fixed rate. We put another $25,000 into the house to fix some issues, replace the roof after a couple of years, and tend to general maintenance. You know, to "protect our investment."

In 2008, we watched our home value plummet. We cringed a bit, but our home was still worth the amount of our mortgage, so we stuck it out. Since then, we have watched our home value crumble, along with the safety of the surrounding neighborhood. Right now, our house is worth about $30,000 less than our mortgage. That $60,000 cash we put into it is long gone, and now we're just renting from the bank. The neighborhood is deteriorating because people can no longer afford the upkeep, and I'm certain the banks won't step in to protect their investments.

We have since learned that the housing market was artificially inflated by banks doling out easy money. Many of those easy mortgages were given to people who had no ability to pay for them; they were preyed upon by unscrupulous lenders. And then those "toxic" mortgages were rolled into AAA securities that eventually killed what were usually very safe bets.

This makes me think the housing crash of 2008 was not an unfortunate accident, but rather the fallout of careless gambling and calculated, short-term greed. We were set up.

I don't expect you to do anything about it. I'd rather you just get out of the way so the rest of the country can start rebuilding. Take your business to Greece, or Ireland. Oh wait, you already bankrupted those countries. I guess the US was just the next target.

John Farley
New Brunswick, NJ 08901

Foreclosure Fairness

I have a friend who was given one of those initial low-interest mortgage loans to buy a house. He did not have a down payment or enough money to repay the loan. A predatory loan company gave him the mortgage without looking at his creditworthiness or bank account balance.

My friend thought he could get by with the initial mortgage payments. He wasn't aware that his payments would increase exponentially and become unaffordable within a year's time, and he defaulted on his payments. Because the bank approved the loan, he thought his creditworthiness was okay and trusted the bank to do the right thing. He has currently lost his home and gone bankrupt. The bank foreclosed on his home and he was homeless for a while. If the bank had done the right thing in the first place and examined his creditworthiness and bank balance, and if the bank had told him that he needed more money to carry a loan like this, then his life would not have been ruined the way it is now.

I am not letting my friend off the hook for his responsibility in this mess, but it is not all his fault. It is the bank's fault for acting predatorily and selling him a mortgage they either knew he couldn't afford or didn't care whether he could afford. Like casinos, the banks bet on the probability my friend would default, and the banks won billions off the backs of people like my friend. And my friend's life is much worse. They won big and he lost very big. This is crazy and absolutely unfair. Balance and regulation must be imposed on the banking/financial industry.

Carole Marcacci
Acton, MA 01720

They Played by the Rules

My beloved parents are struggling. My father worked for HP for over thirty years, and my mother was a special education teacher for the Baltimore City public school system. They have seen their retirement savings disappear and are now fed by a charity food program. My father cheerfully told me that next week they will have fruit to eat again, as they had eaten their last two bananas that morning. I'm crying as I write this.

Someone Else's America . . .

I used to have an America. I shared it with millions. We worked hard, shared the dream, and played by the rules. When we had a problem legislators sat down and negotiated a solution.

Slowly it came to be less and less my America. The lifetime I spent earning my pension wasn't enough. It was said we couldn't afford pensions; they were a mistake America made. Social Security, too, was a mistake. My grandchildren found it harder and harder to get meaningful financial aid for college. Unions were dismantled and millions of jobs went across the water. . . . People hurried in the door of Walmart and dozens and dozens of businesses went away down on Main Street. We no longer had the shared dream. The so-called "job creators" did what they pleased, and the Tea Party wore guns and preached at us from the television. A politician yelled, "You lie!" at our President, and added a million dollars to his coffers in a day just for having done so.

It is almost too late, but we in the middle class want our America back, and we are willing to work to see it happen.

Kathleen Beauchot
Miles City, MT 59301

Wake Up!

Pension Lost in 2008 Crash

You folks should visit my church on any given Sunday afternoon and talk to the seventy or eighty adults (and some children) who show up for a shower, hot meal, and clean clothes. I always think, *There but for the grace of God go I.*

However, these folks were much less fortunate than I: they fell out of the middle class by losing their jobs and their homes. It's amazing to hear the stories of sheer survival. I wonder if their stories would prick your conscience?

Malissa
Santa Fe, NM 87505

How We're Doing Out Here

TO: SUSAN S. BIES, BANK OF AMERICA

Dear Ms. Bies:

I read that a lot of Wall Street executives do not understand why the Occupy Wall Street protesters are doing this. I thought it might help if you knew a little about life in a different part of America.

I live in a small town in Illinois. Years ago there was a manufacturing plant here and a thriving downtown business district. But the manufacturing work moved overseas, where I'm sure it could be done more cheaply, and the plant closed.

Over the years, we have lost most of the local businesses, including both of our grocery stores. In the last few months, the pharmacy and hardware store closed. Our newspaper had to lay off all but one part-time employee. Our school district is in desperate financial straits—they have cut spending so deeply that there is now only one English teacher for the entire high school. And still, the board just received a projection that it will run out of money to operate the schools within two years.

Almost 15% of us are out of work—and that doesn't include many of us who are employed at minimum wage ($8.75/hour) jobs like clerking at Walmart, which is an hour round-trip drive from here with gas at $3.40. More than half of the children at the school qualify for free or reduced lunches because their family incomes are so low. Our food pantry says it served over 10% of the families in our community in the last year. Imagine that you've worked hard all your life and now, with your children watching, you have to line up for a handout at the food pantry.

There are coffee cans on the counter of the convenience store for people with cancer or injured kids without medical insurance. You throw in your change and hope it will help somehow.

Our neighbors, with teenagers our children grew up with, are about to be evicted from their house. Their car was repossessed. Their father works in construction, and there hasn't been much of that going on since the real estate market crashed, which you may remember. Whose fault was that—his? He does any work he can get now, and so does his wife. They can't get enough to keep a roof over their heads.

People have nowhere to live, while houses stand empty. Teachers have been thrown out of work, while the school has no one to teach the kids. The road to the town north of us is closed indefinitely because the bridge is unsafe. We have people in town with the skills to fix it who need the work desperately, but there is no money to pay for it.

I have had the privilege of relatively high-paying work at times in my life, and I know that being comfortable or well-off can insulate a person from the reality that others are not. You're working hard, you feel you deserve to be well paid, and everyone else should just do the same. But that is an easy and false conclusion—most people do not have the opportunity you have been fortunate to receive.

I hope this picture of how some of the other 99% are doing sheds light on what Occupy Wall Street is all about. The enormous disparity of incomes in this country is unjust and growing. People in your world are doing great (from what we hear, "great" doesn't begin to describe it), while the rest of us are going down. It is a disaster and it cannot continue.

Friends and Neighbors

Good day. Since I live in California and know so many who have lost homes and jobs, I wasn't sure who to write. So I chose an investment firm, as I lost so much money in my 457 when the fan was hit.

I will address the loss of neighbors. My mom has lost neighbors on both sides of the family home. One home has been for sale for about two years, while the other was purchased as a short sale by an investor and now has a nice stable public employee owner (hope, hope).

My sister and brother-in-law have three homes across the street from them that have been for sale for about four years and are barely being maintained. Even the squatters don't paint.

I lost some great friends, they lost their home and dreams and marriage to a short sale . . . the bright side being I got equals in the new owners. At least ten other homes around me have been foreclosed, most were rental properties—sorely impacting the tenants as well.

I like meeting new people as does the rest of my family, but mom is elderly and really hates having vacant houses next door.

Must find another pen pal to talk about loss of jobs, so you don't get the pleasure of hearing those stories. Though as head of human capital management, those may mean more to you.

Sick of Being Unemployed and Poor

I have great sympathy for the Occupy Wall Street movement, for I believe that not since the Great Depression has there been such a huge gap between the very wealthy and the struggling, below-poverty-line masses.

Like many in today's economy, at one time my husband and myself, now unemployed seniors, were (lower) middle class at least—we raised three children and met all of their basic needs, although luxuries were limited to movie-going and occasional dining out . . . now we are living in Section 8 housing and are on food stamps, and we still struggle less than our three adult children who make too much money to get any tax breaks or welfare-type relief and yet do not make enough money to pay their bills or break even!

The middle class is "mad as hell and not gonna take it anymore" . . . you think massive, ugly, destructive riots can't happen here in the good ole' USA? Think again . . . if we seniors feel like going out and breaking some windows how do you think angry, disillusioned youth are reacting? I worry, I really do . . . something must be done!

[Name withheld]
Snohomish, WA 98290

Our Mortgage Modification Hardship Letter

To whom it may concern:

As the son of a plumber with fifty years of perspective, and as a plumber himself with thirty-five years of experience, my husband always reassured me that his profession was "recession proof."

He said that in good times there is new construction. In hard times there is the steady need for repairs.

But his work experience and the wisdom of his father did not prepare us for the economic meltdown of the California building and trades industry beginning in 2008.

My own parents told me stories of their struggles in the 1930s and how they lost everything. And only through the creative programs of the Roosevelt Administration were they able to awake from the nightmare of the Great Depression to work for the American Dream. The message was that if you worked hard and saved and were frugal you could raise a family, educate your children, and provide for your retirement.

I began my first job at 14 in a bakery and delicatessen. I worked each summer, after school and on weekends. Later I trained with a designer in high school and was sewing professionally by the time I was 16. My skilled hands and art talents during child-rearing years brought in additional income to augment my husband's steady paycheck.

We wisely invested in a home of our own right from the beginning with a significant down payment nearly twenty-five years ago. Neither of us has ever owned a new car. Bob's skilled hands could put new life into our modest vehicles and we could be content and mobile. Our vacations were usually camping locally except for an occasional motel stay to visit family for a wedding or funeral. Dinner out was saved for birthdays or anniversaries. And we've been to the theatre three times together in twenty-four years. I say all of this with great love and appreciation because we have been very proud and contented that we have found joy in supporting three children into adulthood, and two out of three have completed the college education that neither of us had the privilege to enjoy. And even that was with having raised responsible, ethical children who worked hard to share the burden of their own education. With this record we never figured we would have to ask for assistance to keep our dream alive.

So what happened? Why can't we do this now?

It began slowly. Like most middle-class people our wages did not keep up with the cost of living. As a self-employed contractor, Bob was facing skyrocketing material costs. Gas prices (due to the speculators) hit the roof, a significant burden in rural service work. Insurance costs quadrupled.

The "experts" advised us to "fall back on" the equity in our home. We listened and though reluctant, we were forced to refinance. When we were told not to worry because the value of our home was secure, we listened and believed.

When homeowners ask Bob to assess a plumbing procedure, they depend upon his "expertise" and honesty to help guide them. We did the same with our financial advisors. And I believe that what was told us was said in good faith.

But what has happened in the economy went beyond what responsible people could have known. The recent meltdown could be compared to an in-home plumbing job being very sound. But when the Federal Dam broke upriver and the whole village is under water, then the home owner (mortgage lender) holds the local plumber accountable for the water in his house.

The consequences of the "Federal Dam" began two years ago. New housing stopped. And the phone ringing for service calls—that absolutely stopped. If people had a broken toilet, they stopped using it and availed themselves of the other bathroom. No work. This had never happened as long as I've been a plumber's wife. I used to worry that my husband would work himself to death. We attended several funerals last year of men in the trades. I was told by friends that I needed to tell Bob to slow down and take care of himself as they recognized him as such a hard worker. But honestly, this year I have worried more about him as I watched his blood pressure rise when the work stopped! At the moment some has trickled in but some economists have warned that this is a recession with a recovery in the pattern of a "W" and that we cannot take comfort in the promise of a steady upward shift.

To complicate matters, I was diagnosed with breast cancer four years ago. Having paid into the same insurance company for twenty-one years, as fate would have it, one month before my diagnosis, our plan was changed (due to the fact Bob is the sole proprietor of his company) and the rates skyrocketed while the out-of pocket expenses went off the charts (four shots for $4,000 each, two pills $480, needed four times). These expenses on top of time away from work to be with me through sixteen weeks of chemotherapy, bilateral mastectomy, and seven weeks of radiation took its financial toll and decimated our savings. And though I'm grateful to have survived, the surgery has left me with lymphedema in my left arm and hand. Before the recession I had contributed to our income with my painting skills—fine art and mural work. It only requires the use of my right hand and arm. Since the recession/depression art sales have dried up, I've not had a commission for two years. I can't fall back on my sewing skills as my left hand, used almost as much as my right, is confined to a medical compression sleeve that goes up to my shoulder. And my left fingers lose feeling, cramp up, and turn blue. I even considered going back to the bakery/deli work that I did fifty years ago, but was denied because of sanitary considerations with the rubber glove and sleeve. I will continue to be on oral chemotherapy for two more years.

The cost of this is an incredible burden in an already difficult economic environment. So I'm sorry to have to burden the poor person whose job it is to have to read this. It is not by complaining that we have made it so far.

We have a few things in our favor. We are in the process of creating multiple revenue streams. One is by renting out rooms in our home. If we can save it, we can share it with others, bringing in additional income toward the mortgage. Another is that we are working to rent out a small country cottage to bring in more revenue.

Some work has begun to come in for me and for my husband. We both have had to "earn a degree" in marketing. We are working on a new networking plan and have started a new advertising campaign and website to generate more work and I'm happy to say that there is some improvement. I have a dental office to showcase my mural work in starting next month and Bob has begun to see his work pick up also.

We are hardworking and optimistic people. And so far we have not ever asked for help.

But today we must appeal to you to ask for a modification in our loan in order to continue to stay in our beloved home.

I will leave you with the image of my last painting called "A Vision of Hope and Optimism."

Sometimes a picture says it all. Hopefully this letter will be the seed that will sprout into a better future. Thank you for your attention. God Bless.

Sincerely,

Carol A. Salomon-Bryant & Robert A. Bryant
Petaluma, CA 94954

Banks that Foreclose

Banks that foreclose on family homes often end up trying to sell those properties at a fraction of their worth, simply to avoid paying the taxes that accrue from the property. Seizing a home often costs a bank money, and yet it wreaks havoc on the life of the family the home is being seized from. Leniency in loaning is a practice that we all need to recognize as important in these tough

Carol A. Salomon-Bryant. A Vision of Hope and Optimism.
20" × 48" acrylic (color) on canvas.
See manifestationsonline.com.

times, and yet banks continue to take from the 99%, even when it's not in the best fiscal interest of the bank.

Moreover, charging increased fees to families who are out of work because they are not receiving "direct deposits" or other requirements of free checking or savings accounts is a morally corrupt practice. When people are hurting the most is when you gouge them with the most fees.

I would like to see everyone in America remove their accounts from the big national banks. I know that I will. Perhaps when you don't have the 99% to prey on, you will realize just how important we are to your own livelihoods.

Janell Haynes
Syracuse, NY 13224

Thank You for My Lessons

TO: JAY MANDELBAUM, JP MORGAN CHASE

Dear Jay,

I just wanted to thank you for giving me a mortgage I couldn't afford in 2006. I was naïve. I had never bought a house before; but luckily I had a mortgage broker who was making a large amount of money for securing a very high mortgage for me and my family. You see, we lived in Florida and in 2006, I was afraid if we didn't buy a home immediately, we would be locked out forever. Again, I was young and naïve and didn't understand what it would mean for the "bubble to burst."

My mortgage broker assured me that we had sufficient income to buy this house and the bank agreed. We were making about $50,000 annually as a married couple with one child. Our 1,200 square-foot, two-bedroom, two-bathroom house was $165,000. We thought the right thing to do would be to put our savings into the home and pay 20% down. So that's what we did. We also put $10,000 in upgrades and repairs so we could increase the equity in our home. After all, our home was the safest place to put it, right? It was all relative to the market and the market was doing fantastic. We could even make money off of our home someday. We weren't planning to do this, but what a great option to have. We escrowed our taxes and insurance and our payment was $900 month. A little steep for our modest income, but we were going to make it work no matter what. They also sold us a fifty-year mortgage to lower the payment. But it was a fixed rate and we were told this was what we wanted in order to have a predictable mortgage, so we felt comfortable. After all, we were going to live here forever or for a long time. And in ten or so years, we should have some decent equity in the home and might even be able to sell it.

But then our taxes went up and so did our insurance, and our payment went up to $1,700 month. It was also peculiar that only $15 per month of that amount was going to principal and the rest to interest. That's when I learned that we had a negative amortization loan. We would never really be able to outrun the interest because we would never pay enough on principal. We didn't have anything extra to send in with a $1,700 month payment. Talk about some serious stress at this point. *We'll just cut back*, we thought. We shut off our cable, got rid of our cell phones. Bought cheap food. But we couldn't make it happen.

Two years into the mortgage, and after our mortgage had been sold three times, we asked for a loan modification. We were told we weren't behind in payments, so we had to stop sending them. The representative said we should save those payments because we would use them for a new down payment when we were approved for the modification. So we did exactly as we were told. But, once we were assigned to a modification case-worker, we could never get her on the phone. Ever. It took six months for first contact. Then, we were served foreclosure papers.* I begged and pleaded and frantically reminded the call center representatives every day that we had only done what we were told. I advised we had saved all of the payments and had six months' worth of payments in the bank that I would hand over now. They said they could not accept payments on a property in foreclosure.

We hired an attorney and they eventually offered to modify the loan after a couple of years of fighting it, but we would also owe $8,000 in their attorney's fees. We were not willing to do this, since we had only done what they advised us to do. We realized later that we had a mortgage servicer, who was on your side, Mr. Bank Official, not ours. So, we were treated like criminals every

---

* As is documented in the National Mortgage Settlement of 2012, misleading advice was often given to holders of mort-gages that they needed to be sixty days delinquent in pay-ments to qualify for a loan modification — one element of banks' and lenders' widespread fraud and abuse in loan modi-fication proceedings. See Appendix B.

time we talked to someone at the servicer. You were, after all, the servicer's client. I was not.

Our home has been worth $60,000 since 2008. We put down $30,000, completed $10,000 in upgrades in the first year and paid $40,000 in payments in the first two years before the modification mess occurred. Our total investment: $80,000. The house is worth $60,000 and we now owe more than we financed due to late fees, attorney's fees, and mortgage payments. We have been forced into bankruptcy because there is no other option at this point. Sure, one of the many servicers that have managed our loan has offered us a modification, but we would have to sign our rights to bankruptcy away, pay their attorney's fees, and accept many other conditions that our attorneys have advised us to not agree to.

We take responsibility for not educating ourselves more before we entered into the very serious contract of mortgaging a home. We wish the industry would have taken this contract much more seriously as well. If they had, they would have denied us the loan, knowing very well that we would not be able to sustain the payments long-term. I also wish there were requirements such as classes that better explain things like what a rise in escrow cost might mean for the bottom line of your mortgage payment. We must have asked twenty times at closing what our final payment would be and we were told over and over: $900. We were never told that our exemptions were different than those of the widow who sold us the home, so our escrow would increase for the negative amount as well as an additional collection to pad for the following year. But we should have researched more before entering into such a serious agreement

Thank you again for ruining our financial life. We have gained much experience, and for that we are thankful. We know that owning an overpriced mortgage on a devalued home is not our American Dream. We know that we will never borrow money from anyone for anything ever again. We know that our possessions do not define us, but our ability to survive and learn and love does.

We know that we are blessed to have jobs and families that love us. We know that we are so sorry you could not take our payments when you made a mistake because we wanted to honor our debts, even if it was a nightmare situation. Most of all, we know that we will be okay because our money and possessions do not define us, but our integrity and compassion do. We wish the same for you and your employees and hope you can someday learn the lessons we have.

Hello, Edith

TO: EDITH W. COOPER, GOLDMAN SACHS

I certainly hope you are well. I remember in February of 2008 when you were speaking at the HBS Women's Association of Greater New York. You remember, don't you? You spoke about "Finding Balance in Investing, Work and Life." How wonderful for you. I mean, in light of the fact that you apparently hadn't a clue.

Long ago, at least two decades ago, a very wise old woman spoke to me about balance. She was old, Edith. Her face was as lined as those old puckered apple dolls that children and their grandmothers used to make. She was poor in the way of material things, as many wise old ones are. But her eyes sparkled with both kindness and a sense of humor. She spoke of what a great thing it was that women had moved out into the workplace as highly educated participants in what had once been an all-male domain.

She felt it to be an empowering thing overall, but issued, also, a warning. A caveat of sorts. She said that women hold a sacred responsibility (those were her words, Edith), and that those women who moved into that once all-male domain ran the risk of forgetting what their sacred responsibility was. That women tend to accommodate the males around them. This is neither good or bad. It is just a woman's way. But that if she accommodated too much in the testosterone-laden atmosphere she would forget her true power, and trade it in for the power of becoming "an apprenticed male."

Well, I of course asked her to speak more and to explain. And she said that women carry a greater capacity for compassion. For empathy. For seeing the interconnectedness between people and within systems. And we're better able to consider the effects upon children, elders, and the infirm, in most decision-making processes. Being in the highly competitive arenas that were once male-only can often cut a woman off from the very traits any culture needs. For what is a culture without compassion? Without empathy? Without a recognition of our interconnectedness? Interesting.

Goldman Sachs, which you have obviously thought a great place to work, couldn't even balance its books. Goldman Sachs required a bailout from the 99% to the tune of $63.6 billion. And even though that was the case, Goldman Sachs reported profits for 2009–2010 in the $21.7 billion range. Yet, Goldman Sachs has made political contributions, in excess of $8.4 million, which appears to be a bit dodgy, doesn't it? Not to mention the frank and outright lobbying Goldman Sachs has done . . . another $11.2 million.

Perhaps, Edith, you would do well to contemplate the topic of balance a bit more. To help you with this here are some other words: Balance. Harmony. Proportion. Symmetry. These are the things that are missing at Goldman Sachs. And were stolen from the people of our great nation, Edith. Indeed they were stolen from every country involved in our global economy. It is time to wake up, Edith. Sleep is done now. Wake up. Wake up. Wake up.

Sincerely, The 99%

B. Soutar
Woodstock, GA 30188

I Have Worked in Corporate America

Gentlemen,

I have worked in corporate America. I have run my own small business. I truly understand how hard you have to work and the responsibility you have to your shareholders. In many ways, running a company is similar to caring for a child.

However . . .

There has been a skewing of priorities over the last thirty years toward the belief that profits are all that matter and that everyone connected to the machine that garners those profits is lucky to be employed and getting a paycheck. Also, that the people driving the ship should become super-rich because the company grosses $X billions per year. This, in my opinion, is not American. In America, everyone is supposed to have a chance to work hard, earn a decent wage, and provide a comfortable life for themselves and their families.

Somewhere along the line, private jets, villas in the south of France, and a penthouse on the Upper East Side became the tip of the iceberg for the C-suite in America.

I know you are not all money-grubbing heartless bastards who think the little people should "eat cake." I've worked with you; I've observed you interacting with your employees and your peers. For the most part, you're all decent people.

Please wake up and realize that the average guy on the street is not a lazy, stupid fool who has squandered the same opportunities you've had and gotten himself stuck on the bottom rung of the social classes. Most Americans on "Main Street" do work hard . . . really hard, to provide for their families, watch what they spend, and raise their kids with morals and values so they can be productive members of society. Are there going to be abuses of social programs? Always. Are social programs abused by the majority of the people receiving benefits, or people just trying to pay their mortgage? Absolutely not.

Maybe you personally didn't cause the economy to tank in '08, but you know as well as I do that you had a pretty good idea of what was going on. The US taxpayers bailed out the banks, but the banks are not lending, so small businesses can't get loans. Hell, some large businesses can't get the credit they need.

There was a time when the stock market was people making educated bets on which company's true value was going to rise and fall, and they invested as they saw fit. Now it has nothing to do with value: it has to do with finding an angle, exploiting the rules, and beating the quarterly earnings predictions—damn the consequences!

Please take this opportunity to show your humanity. Lead your companies in an ethical way. Earn a healthy, sustainable return for your shareholders instead of a huge "score" built on smoke and mirrors. In the end, America will thank you for it, and you will thank yourselves.

Sincerely,

Jamie Gannon
Plainview, NY 11803

I Pray for Your Well-Being

As a psychotherapist and former school counselor, I am well aware that children and adults who behave heartlessly toward others have themselves been treated in a heartless manner; that bullies have themselves been bullied; that greed is a sign of deep emotional pain. I see these signs of deep emotional pain in you. I pray for your emotional wounds to heal so that you can reunite with your own caring, loving sense of connection to the world and all its inhabitants and use your strengths, your passion, and your drive to benefit all of the world, not just the 1% of people who are also as wounded as you are. I am a very skilled therapist and would gladly work with you either in my office in NYC or via phone or Skype. I believe that together we could break through your defenses and help you live a much happier, healthier life. Sincerely.

I Worked in Banking for Thirty Years

I worked in Banking for thirty years. I was a VP at one NYC bank in the '80s. It was a fabulous company. At some point a new CEO was hired. This person helped destroy the Bank with bottom-line everything. During one year, all salaries were frozen (I did not have a problem with that) to help the bottom line. Some employees who performed above goals were rewarded with stock options since no bonuses or salary increases could be given. After I left that Bank, I exercised much of my options and coupled with part of my 401(k) that was in stock, felt secure with my decision and rewards for working hard and achieving my goals.

Fast-forward and that Bank was bought by another Bank. Stock prices for many years grew steadily. Then the President/CEO got greedy. The Bank played games with no-doc mortgages, fancy loan bundling, drive-by inspections, etc. The president was the darling of Wall Street. Meanwhile, cracks in the strategy were starting to appear. Senior people with morals alerted top executives that the bottom was falling out. They were ignored or fired. Worse, employees were assured all was OK. Then the crash came quickly. There was a run on the Bank and as I was told, refusal by the president to merge. A potential buyer approached by the government played hardball and in the blink of an eye, the Bank was seized by the FDIC. Shareholders lost everything. Then the same greedy buyer who refused the deal turned around and bought the Bank for pennies.

I and many of my former employees lost all of our stock. These CEOs of both banks made millions and then went on with no punishment for anything they had done while they destroyed the lives of so many people.

To claim that the 99 percenters are wrong, that many top Wall Street and Banking executives are not crooks or elites, and that no crimes were committed, is false. Those who cheated deserve to be in jail along with some of their immediate families who not only benefited financially but then claimed ignorance. Sadly, this will never be made right. I left Banking because I could no longer justify or stomach the behavior of those top executives. Some of my friends who are still in Banking tell me they are expected to sell their soul if they want to keep their job. Disgusting!

How Do You Sleep at Night?

TO: HEIDI MILLER, JP MORGAN CHASE

Are you sleepwalking your way through life? Wake up, Heidi! I am your friend, I love you!

This is my story. I live in a one-bedroom apartment with my daughter. I am 30 years old and I have been working for over twelve years. I have had to change occupations three times in the last decade because I was laid off and/or the company I worked for closed. I worked in your call centers and collected debts for you, calling people at home and at work collecting money for you. Then you closed my office.

I make $11/hour and that is too much to get assistance like food stamps, or even assistance with my power bill. I feed my daughter first. I buy her clothes and shoes as she continues to grow up fast. I want to have a computer and the internet to be informed and participate in this century. I do not have even basic cable. My rent is just $400 because I have the most run-down apartment in my city. It's all I can afford. I never have over $200 in my bank account.

And yet you want more from me?! How do I pay you, Heidi? My daughter deserves a chance to someday go on a vacation. She cannot because I cannot afford to fix our car or even fill up the tank. I walk her to daycare. My daughter deserves the same opportunities you had. How can you take that from her? Who will replace you? Our children are very bright and it is our job to nurture this.

What do I tell her when she wants to go to college? "First, you must pay Heidi's interest. To pay that, you must work full-time and starve"?! "You will never be more than the working poor thanks to our friend Heidi and her network of bankers"? "You beautiful, smart, bright genius must pay Heidi back your entire life. Neither you nor I will ever own homes or have yards to garden. But Heidi and her friends love you so pay them"?! Is this what I tell her?

Wake up, Heidi, we love you.

From a Fellow Capitalist

I'm a capitalist too. I own a small hair salon in Manhattan. But we have made investments to minimize the harm our company does. We pay more for our electricity because we want to use wind power and encourage investment in alternative energy. We pay more for organic products so that we minimize the chemicals on our skin, in the air, and in the water supply. We want to make a profit and meet our financial obligations, but we want to do so with a clear conscience.

It pains me to see big businesses garnering advantages in government and benefitting from bailouts, subsidies, and tax loopholes while we watch our costs and credit rates increase and our customers' ability to pay for services decline.

Please tell me it pays to be honest and ethical. Please join our fight for equity in governmental representation and better terms for all businesses—not just the big ones—because we will all benefit.

Caroline Holley
Brooklyn, NY 11201

Bank of America

About as Mainstream as You're Going to Get

A *New York Times* article said that the Wall Street CEOs think we're a bunch of fringe lunatics. I'm about as mainstream as you're going to get. A civil servant with a professional title. I get 0.75% on my savings, and pay so many banking fees for the privilege of having you guys use my money that I'd be ahead keeping my money in my mattress. I have a credit rating of 790, but that didn't stop B of A from raising my Visa rate from 7.5% to 12.5% to pay for, according to their explanation, "fines and penalties." Yeah, B of A's fines and penalties. This, after taking my tax dollars in bailouts. I'm not fringe. I'm just mad as hell.

Ilene S.
New York City

Greetings from a Soon-to-Be Ex-B of A Customer

TO: RON D. STURZENEGGER, BANK OF AMERICA

Ron:

My name is Elizabeth Lang. I am a B of A customer in Westlake Village, CA. I have been a customer for a very long time, and not only are my personal bank accounts and my mortgage with Bank of America, my small business banking and credit line are with B of A, too.

Several months ago, I noted that Bank of America had started withdrawing approximately $90 per month from my bank account. I had never approved any such automatic withdrawal, so I called your customer service line and learned from a fairly unfriendly customer service representative that it was for "homeowners insurance."

The rep claimed that I had failed to prove I had homeowners insurance, so B of A had started taking the money from my account—without telling me.

Here's the rub. I have had the same homeowners insurance policy since I purchased my home. The last time I checked, randomly taking money from my account constitutes *theft*. So my next step was to head to my branch of B of A to speak to someone in person.

Upon arriving at my bank branch and requesting to speak to a manager, I was told, "you are not allowed to speak to a manager." Flabbergasting. My own bank is stealing my money and I'm "not allowed" to speak to a bank manager in person? While I did (after hours of talking with rude, unhelpful customer service reps) manage to get my money refunded, I am still disgusted.

Cut to three weeks ago when I went to my bank to deposit some checks. The line for the ATM was too long—so I opted to go inside to the completely empty bank where tellers stood around doing nothing. Upon completing my transaction, the teller said, "You have a large balance, you should consider opening a money market account that would earn interest for you." My response? Wondering how my opening a money market account would benefit B of A—because you certainly aren't trying to do me any favors or earn me interest.

That's when I realized . . . *I don't trust you.* You stole from me in the past. You push us all on the ATMs then charge us to use them. Your customer service consists of surly, churlish and unhelpful people.

In short, I'm leaving and taking my "large balance" and my good credit rating and I'm going to a local credit union where I suspect I won't be treated like chattel.

I'm sending this email to you and a number of your colleagues. I challenge just one B of A executive to respond to me personally and tell me why I should stay at your institution.

Sincerely,

Elizabeth Lang
Westlake Village, CA 91362

How You Have Screwed Me Over

My husband and I have a small business, and at one time we employed nine people including ourselves. In order to keep our business going, we took equity out of our house three times. This helped pay salaries and improved the business.

Then the bubble you helped create burst and got crap all over us. We could still manage to pay our employees, but not ourselves. We were having a hard time making our mortgage payments, so we asked B of A if we could get a loan modification. These were supposed to be available at the time. We were told that we would not be considered if we were making payments. So we stopped making payments and started the procedure. We sent in papers, you lost the papers. We sent in papers again, you couldn't find them again. Finally, you said that you had the papers. We called every week, and no one knew what was going on. In the meantime, we were cutting costs in our business. This meant having to let go of people and many other measures. We gutted our retirements, sold our second car and some gold coins. I am now 69 years old with no savings whatsoever. My husband doesn't have any, either.

Eventually we were approved, then we weren't approved. We kept calling. Each call took at least half an hour to find the right department, even though we always called the last department that we had spoken to. Most didn't know anything about our request. This went on for over eighteen months. Every day we are living with the fear of losing our home. No one knows what is going on. We are given contradicting advice from the bank; people are gone, people don't call back. We finally get the dreaded foreclosure notice, even though we have spoken to someone almost every week trying to resolve this. Then we have to get a lawyer, which costs a lot of money we don't have, but *I'm not going to lose my home.* I can't sleep, my husband can't sleep. And yet, you get bonuses and live in the lap of luxury while thousands of people are in pure misery.

Thank you.

Penelope Sallberg-Carrillo
Pasadena, CA 91104

Time for Change

It's depressing to see how things have ended up this way. When I was in the military, we were encouraged to open accounts with B of A and I presumed that meant it was safe. Shortly thereafter, in my first financial solo situation, I lost thousands of dollars to fees, bounces, and generally not being very good at understanding the twenty-four hold and my debit card. I chose not to take part in the class-action suit as I think suits aren't necessary and generally don't do any good anyway . . . but I never banked with you again. I took the losses as my own growing pains and kept going. Banks and big corporations have the power to change things. To turn the other cheek without strictly worrying about the bottom line makes a difference. . . . Don't you think it's time for a little change?

Bernadine Turner
Newberry, FL 32669

Insurance Fraud

Dear Bank of America and affiliates,

Since my mortgage was bought by good old B of A I am required to carry flood insurance for over twice what my property is worth. If I can't get my own, B of A will purchase it for me, for about twice what I have to pay my current insurance company. Last year it took me three months to get the money together and B of A charged me $600 for retroactive coverage plus interest. I am 68 years old and retired. My property is now appraised at less than what I owe on it. I am barely hanging on and B of A is apparently eager to see me go down.

By the way, they would not refinance my property because it is not a "conventional structure" but they want me to carry flood insurance of over $200,000. Who is getting rich off of this and how do they get away with it? There has not even been a claim for flood damage since the home was built in the '70s. If I go under I plan to move to the B of A parking lot in town with my four dogs and three cats.

Jimmie Oneal
Meadow Valley, CA 95956

Greetings from Detroit!

TO: CHRISTINE P. KATZIFF, BANK OF AMERICA

Dear Christine:

I would like to personally invite you to Detroit! Have you ever been here? It's a lovely town—of course, we have a B of A on every corner! Why, many of my friends have done business with your good friends over at Countrywide Insurance! I know, it's a small world! So, you'd be more than welcome to take a tour of our beautiful town and its lovely neighborhoods.

Oh, what's that you say? You've heard Detroit is actually not a very nice place? You've heard that many of the homes in Detroit are foreclosed on at higher rates than in other American cities? Well, I guess you're right about that. After all, most people who live in Detroit are African-American, and Bank of America surely knows that African-Americans are losing their homes faster than white people (though there are plenty of white people losing their homes, too—so obviously you don't discriminate *too* much!).* Anyway, Detroit used to be a really nice place to live. And lots of people would like to buy homes in Detroit and fix them up and make them pretty again, but Bank of America and Countrywide

---

* The Federal Government in 2011 charged Bank of America's subsidiary Countrywide with systematic racial discrimination in mortgage lending, leading to a $335 million settlement for the 200,000 minority borrowers identified as victims. The lender put African-American and Latino borrowers into riskier subprime loans than their white peers with identical credit, and charged the minority borrowers higher interest and fees. See Appendix B.

probably wouldn't stand to make too much money if houses sold cheaply and mortgages were fair and banks were more flexible when the unemployment rate in America is around 9% (here in Detroit, it's more like 14%—that's really high, in case you didn't know).

So, Christine! Come visit us here in Mo-Town! Why, we'd be happy to show you what it's like to lose your home even in one of the most sparsely populated cities with tremendous issues around blight, abandoned homes, and deteriorating housing stock. I mean, really! You might get a kick out of it! Or you might decide to make a conscious, ethical decision to advocate for the 99%—the ones that make your world go 'round.

Love and Hugs from Motor City!

Fritz
Detroit, MI 48238

Mortgage Fraud

When I refinanced my mortgage in 2006 with Countrywide, I did so to get my payment down. The guy I spoke with sold me on taking out some of the equity on my house to get my kitchen floors redone and do some repairs on the subflooring that I otherwise couldn't afford. What I didn't know was that he was going to inflate the property assessment of my home, lie and say that my father also lived at my house so the loan would be approved, and put me in a Pay Option ARM that caused over $10,000 in negative amortization. I was told to pay the minimum payment because that was the interest-only payment, but it wasn't. Now my house is upside down and I am struggling each month to keep afloat. I can't join any of the modification programs that Bank of America (who now services my loan) offers because I haven't fallen behind on my payments, and I refuse to fall behind on my payments because I am trying to maintain a good credit score. If this refinance had not been approved and I had not been misled about the mortgage I was being put into, I would not be in the mess I am in now.

This isn't the last you will hear from me. I am meeting with the state's attorney this week about this.

Jennifer Mercer
Great Mills, MD 20636

Scam by Bank of America

Several years ago, I received an unsolicited call from B of A offering me cash to put in my checking account at 0%. After some cajoling, I accepted $500. When I got my first bill, the interest rate was 25% and a late fee was added. I went straight to a B of A branch and sat for two hours. The late fee was waived. I went over to the teller and immediately paid the balance off. Two days later, the previous month's bill arrived. Had that bill come first, I would have had the promised 0% rate!

Aaron Libson
Philadelphia, PA 19141

Bad Faith Foreclosures

Bank Of America assured a friend that they were working to modify his loan while they were actually moving to foreclose; he was saved only by the intervention of a US senator. Our banks act like a corporate mafia worthy of a RICO indictment.

Ray Kenny
Lake Oswego, OR 97035

My Mortgage

TO: CHARLES O. HOLLIDAY JR, BANK OF AMERICA

Dear Mr. Holliday,

I write to tell you of my late, lamented Bank of America mortgage. I used to live in Phoenix, Arizona. Just after the height of the beautiful balloon ride of a price bubble in Phoenix, my wife and I found a house in Phoenix—it was priced right—so we bought it.

It needed work, but I knew that going in. I used my overtime money to make repairs, paint, and strive to make a lawn grow. About five years later, the economic downturn—made possible by your bank and others engaging in shady financial instruments at a rate of risk that would make a racetrack tout blush—created circumstances that made it necessary to relocate to Salt Lake City, Utah.

We didn't want to go—but if I didn't I would lose my job with USPS—and I had about fifteen years in there. So I did what was expected. I called Bank of America to tell them what was going on. At that time I requested a "deed in lieu of foreclosure." I was instructed that I first must list the house for sale for ninety days.

I called my realtor and he listed my house. Only five days after we listed and we had already left for Salt Lake City, my realtor received a decent short-sale offer, and he informed Bank of America. Well, your company just couldn't make up its mind whether to accept or reject the offer. For more than five months Bank of America skulked around, never saying "no," threatening us with foreclosure but never following through, agreeing to send me a "deed in lieu," but never doing it. Creating a financial limbo around the property and ultimately putting the property at risk.

You see, I had some acquaintances looking after the place. They began to report to me that folks were breaking in and squatting there. This happened at least three times. One occasion resulted in the Phoenix Police coming to get the people out and the officer had to draw his weapon. Inside were two people, with furniture and everything, including a flat screen TV.

At long last, Bank of America made up its collective mind to say yes to the offer, and the buyer took a last walk through. The place had been vandalized by then, and the buyer said no.

I still have not received a "deed in lieu." As far as we know we haven't even been foreclosed upon. Since corporations are now people, will you please call up this person who has such a ridiculous name as Bank of America and tell him or her about this? Because maybe this person will take pity on me and my wife. I mean he or she does exist, right? And if he or she does, he or she must have some sense of common decency or basic compassionate feeling.

If you want, I'll be glad to go see him or her and we will chat. Does Bank play golf? Maybe I could play a round with Mr. or Ms. Bank—because I am certain if I ever get to meet this guy or girl, I can make him or her see the light and decide to do the right thing. If he or she is any kind of person at all, I am sure that he or she will understand that the smart business move isn't always the right thing to do.

You should probably understand that also, I mean, really, after all it's people like me who bailed you out, and without me I think Mr. or Ms. Bank of America would have been so irked at you, you wouldn't have your job anymore. So let me know what you think—maybe me and you and Mr. or Ms. Bank of America can do lunch.

Almost Three Years Trying to Get a Mortgage Modification

My husband and I work in the entertainment industry and at the end of 2008, the amount of work we were able to find began to fall off. Then I was laid off from two side jobs. We began to hear that we could call Bank of America for help with our mortgage because we realized things might get worse.

We started calling in December of 2008, even though we were current on our loan payments. No one could help us at all for months, and eventually we could no longer make the full payment. At that point, someone we happened to talk to said, "OK, then, based on your income, pay this amount." Which we did. I faxed in all the necessary financial information to be put in a trial modification program through Making Home Affordable. However, over the next year, I kept being put in the program and then mysteriously kicked out. The faxes that I was told were received were suddenly lost a few weeks later. The fax numbers would change and I *never* once, in almost three years now of calling, spoke to the same person twice in the Workout Department, or whatever they call it on the day I call. Finally, in the spring of 2010, we were put into a trial modification program . . . and we finally seemed to be making progress.

However, even though we went through the three-month trial just fine, paying on time, we received no notification of it being made permanent. We continued to pay the trial amount for six more months until we received notice that we were not approved for a permanent modification. That was a huge blow to us. In the meantime, the value of our property has fallen to about half of what we owe.

In June of this year we filed for bankruptcy, but of course that does not affect our mortgage. Foreclosure proceedings have begun, but I am applying once more to Making Home Affordable since our income has come back some. We have lost everything we put into our home and more because Wall Street decided to play games and gamble with the loans of so many people like us. Yet the banks got huge bailouts. Did they use any of that money to help people stay in their homes? No. It's a sad, disgusting and un-American situation.

Julie Sanford
Van Nuys, CA 91406

Taking Advantage of the Disabled

I am currently, but will soon no longer be, a Bank of America customer. I am totally blind and use adaptive technology to read, operate a computer, and print. Bank of America limits wire transfers to $1,000 without pass-through. Their pass-through system is not accessible to us, even with adaptive technology. As a result, in order to transfer $4,000 I have to give the bank an extra $75 or pay for a cab and use sighted assistance to withdraw the cash from my branch which is fifteen minutes away.

I have repeatedly discussed the issue with customer service personnel but they refuse to fix it. My new bank has no limits on wire transfers and no pass-through.

It is unconscionable for this company, which received taxpayer bailout funds and which should be subject to the civil rights laws of the United States and many states and local jurisdictions, to pad its already obscene profits by taking advantage of the disabled.* A teenager who steals a few dollars worth of goods from a convenience store can end up with a long prison term under a draconian law, but no one seems to care if these corporate fat cats break the law.

---

* In an unrelated action in 2012, the Department of Justice and Department of Housing and Urban Development brought charges against Bank of America for discrimination against the disabled in mortgage lending, which the bank settled with payments to each affected applicant who could be identified. See Appendix B.

We Thought We Were Going to Be Alright. . . Until:

In 1991 my family and I arrived in this country. We were blessed with Resident Alien status and worked hard.

We bought a house to live in and raised our children.

We bought another house to rent out for some extra income.

All was well until things started to crash. Renter moved out, work became scarce (I make luxury yachts for you), we were forced into foreclosure by Bank of America who then sold the property to a nice man from the Deutsche Bank on the courthouse steps for *one hundred dollars.*

How much bailout money did B of A receive?

B of A then sold our bad debt to some collection agency for $5,000 who now want $154,000 from me.

Until now we have been able to pay our bills, reduce our debt and put our children through college without financial aid or student loans.

Not any more. I will declare bankruptcy before I pay you greedy weasels one cent.

Florence

Dear Bank of America,

My neighbor has been very good. She paid her bills. She keeps her house and yard better than *House Beautiful*. She didn't lose her job. You mortgaged her at a high rate. All she asked you to do is remortgage her at a reasonable one with no adjustable rate. Why can't you do that?

Why do you want her to put money into an escrow and not tell her how much of that is interest/principal/etc.?

Why do you hate my neighbor? We here in West Seattle really like her; she is a good neighbor.

Her house is nice, small but nice. If you plan to take her house as you say you do and try to live in it yourself, I will teach my dog to poop on your lawn.

Also we are moving our money out of your bank. I am paying off my little loan so you can't make any more profit from me to spend fighting her. I am asking everyone to take their business from your bank. You are very bad people.

PS: Santa is watching, you know.

Chase

I Support Occupy Wall Street

Show your patriotism and pay your fair share of taxes. Show us you differ from the robber barons at the turn of the 20th century.

JP Morgan Chase Investments illegally manipulated my aging mother, who is deaf, into signing papers she did not understand. They did this to move her assets into a different account so they could get their fees for doing so. As a consequence, my mother lost thousands. Of course, that's no skin off their noses; their profitable fees are safe. They also refused her request to close an account—twice—also resulting in a loss of thousands. They are bums for whom I have no respect.

I have to schedule time into my daily routine to argue with bankers. It's absurd.

I figured I'd done everything right. I studied hard, went to a public university, kept out of debt, graduated cum laude, worked full time for twenty-five years, lived frugally, delayed marriage, married another hardworking college graduate, remained married for twenty-two years so far, delayed childbirth, limited children to two . . . and yet. My salary has never equaled, let alone surpassed that of either of my parents (a teacher of English as a second language and a retail sales clerk), neither of whom graduated from college. Our living standards are far lower than those of my parents. We have minimal health insurance; it's all we can afford. We rent, we do not own a home. We've never owned a car younger than fifteen years old. My company folded, and I'm left with no retirement.

Despite a willingness to take on any work (I worked for the 2010 Census), I've been searching for full-time work for over three years. I do piecemeal gigs to try to stay afloat. I work unpaid internships in the hopes of making contacts and landing a job. My husband works four jobs. We now work seven days a week, day and night, no vacations, and have been doing so since 2008. Our two children, who rarely see us anymore, are both honor students. But I worry we won't be able to send them to college. Is this the American dream?

You Already Took One Home from Me, Now You're Working on Another One!

I lost my home to Chase last year. Thanks to the actions of bankers, like you, who caused the mortgage meltdown, the value of my home plummeted to half of its value at the time I purchased it.

Because my income also plummeted due to the recession, you wouldn't qualify me for a mortgage modification. Instead, you chose to accept an offer in a short sale for less than a third of what I owed on it.

You could have lowered my principal to that amount—but instead put me out on the street.

Luckily, I was able to take my child and move in with my boyfriend—now my fiancé—who is now in the *exact same situation*!

He is a businessman whose business has also taken a hit in this economy. He's had business troubles before but has successfully rebuilt his business twice, with no doubts that he'll do so again.

But *you* refuse to work with him on a mortgage modification. The home—with a $560,000 mortgage—is now worth around $325,000. You'd rather put us all out on the street than work with him to lower the payments so that we can stay here?

You are the 1%. He used to be there with you, but never treated others the way you're treating us. Shame on you. You *can* do the right thing by us and others. Grow a conscience, please!

Hey Heidi!

TO: HEIDI MILLER, JP MORGAN CHASE

I've always liked that name. Anyhow, it's your best friend here. *New best friend*, that is. Are you really a JP Morgan exec? And a woman? Don't get me wrong, I'm a feminist all the way, it's just usually companies that are trying to screw the poor aren't usually all about gender equality.

I'm sure you put up with a lot of crap to get where you are. I'm sure at one point almost everyone you work with has baselessly questioned your rise to such a position. I'm sure you had to fight tooth and nail, and deal with people telling you to "smile."

Heidi, you probably think I'm going to be upset with you for being an exec at a company that helped tank the economy and screwed up my future/present. But you are wrong. I've been groped as a waitress, so I can't *imagine* what you have been through, and you know what—keep the money Heidi. That's right—keep it. Let's face it, token women do not get to call the shots at this company anyways. I know that. You know that. So what should you do? Raise all hell, get fired, lose your job, and then have to ask a man for money and/or help? No, no, no.

Dear Heidi and all female execs, I have decided to forgive you for your silence in this catastrophe—because "the man" would not have listened to you anyways, and all that I ask is please leave the money to your daughters. Your sons will have enough of an edge.

Closing My Account on Monday Morning

TO: HEIDI MILLER, JP MORGAN CHASE

Dear Heidi,

After seeing the video of customers being arrested while trying to close their accounts, I have decided that I can no longer do business with your bank. Now that I have learned that your bank has also been funding the violence in New York and donating money to the police, I will be closing my account and moving my money to a credit union. I would like your assurance that I will not be arrested for closing my account.

Have a nice day!

Tax Credits Aren't for Outsourcing

From July 1, 2008 until May 18, 2010, I worked for JP Morgan Chase. I was hired through a temp service to do internal IT support over the phone. When hired, I was told that if I kept my statistics down (first call resolution and call times) that I would eventually be hired as an actual employee. Despite my statistics consistently ranking in the top ten of all of employees in my department, not just the other temps, after two years I was not only *not* hired, I was laid off. Meanwhile, during that two years, other temps with stats much worse than mine were hired.

The reason for my not being hired was never explained to me. It could have been the fact that I am in a wheelchair, and Chase didn't want a disabled woman bringing up their insurance rates. Or perhaps it is because I am a lesbian and, other than myself, there was only one other homosexual in the department who was actually an employee—who was also laid off at the same time as me.

The whole "come work for us and we will eventually give you a great job with awesome benefits" was just a scheme. In 2008, Chase received a state tax credit from Ohio; in return, they were to create 1,200 new jobs within the state. So what did they do? They hired a bunch of temporary employees, got their tax credit, and kept the temporary employees on staff long enough to not only retain their tax credit, but to also set up their call center in the Philippines. Then two years later, they laid off hundreds of people, causing the state to lose more jobs than they had gained during that two year period. Other internal IT departments were outsourced to Mexico and the credit card fraud department was exported to India. Though you surely know all of this.

So through a loophole in the system, your company left more people in our state unemployed and still took taxpayer money to stuff your own pockets, under the guise of being a company creating more jobs. Outsourcing hurts our nation's economy. As a bank in the United States, you would think that you would want people here to have jobs so they could have money to put in your bank.

The Gray Family is the 99%

TO: WILLIAM H. GRAY III, JP MORGAN CHASE

Mr. William Gray,

I thought I'd write to you because we share the same last name and it's during these times of trouble that families need to stick together. The rest of the clan sends their love.

This year, Boyfriend and I decided to move in together. Mom and Dad love him and he's just the kindest, most hardworking guy alive. He ran into some trouble earlier this year when Chase notified him that he would be charged a monthly fee for his checking account unless he had at least one direct deposit transaction per month of over $500. Boyfriend works for UPS and gets paid once a week. None of those paychecks are over $500 because he works part-time so he can finish his Master's degree in English Literature. He wants to be a high school teacher. I, on the other hand, make a bit more than he does and get paid every other week. My directly deposited paychecks are each over $500, so my Chase account is not charged the fee. Of the two of us, Boyfriend makes less money but is charged more. That doesn't seem fair. He can't afford the fee.

So, Boyfriend and I have decided to leave Chase Bank. We don't like your business practices. We don't like that you took federal bailout money ("federal" means "from the taxpayers," i.e. 99% of Americans) and then proceeded to charge people that take home ("take home" in case you didn't know, means "after payroll taxes." We are taxpayers!) $20,800 a year to hold on to their own money.

So, we're switching to a local credit union and telling our family (that's you, Mr. Gray!), friends, neighbors and co-workers to do the same.

Shame on JP Morgan Chase.

The Gray Family is the 99%.

Your Cousin

Our Going on a Year Loan Modification Attempts with Chase

We have lost our high-end design hardware business. We have lost both our mother and mother-in-law after being their caregivers. Our home is definitely valued at much less than it was. My husband is 57 and has tried to find other employment and cannot even get an interview.

Nevertheless, he is slowly getting back on his feet with constant diligence. We have a home that we could work out something reasonable with you to stay in . . . if only you would stop losing our paperwork, our appraisal, changing the people we deal with and your rules, making it harder than it has to be. We deserve better than this bureaucratic game of wearing us down.

We want to pay our mortgage. One that works for us and for you. The months we missed we cannot recover right now but we can start anew and put it on the back end. We had great credit and now we don't. Where else could we go but to the streets? I am 62 and do not want that to be my retirement legacy. Please work with us. We want to work with you.

Thank you for listening,

Barbara and Bruce Gustafson
Santa Monica, CA 93546

Never Again

Dear sirs,

Nearly three years ago, I called your staff to discuss payment options on my two Chase credit cards. I was willing to make some kind of deal to allow me to get the biggest bang for my monthly payments on both cards. Those payments were killing my hopes of having some kind of emergency retirement cash . . . the "just in case" kind of money I'd need as I considered retiring in two years at age 62. I couldn't find anyone with the authority to make any deals with me at the numbers listed either on the back of both cards or the numbers listed on my monthly statements. I gave up and continued to borrow from one card to pay the other until my debt was simply too large. After two and a half years of soul searching, I finally declared bankruptcy. I thought the Chase credit card offers would stop. They didn't, but I did. I would never accept another offer from your bank if you were the last bank on earth. It's too bad your bank won't have the kind of label I'll have associated with my name for the next ten years.

You guys suck!

Betty Wilson
Manhattan, NY 10031

I Miss My Democracy

TO: DAVID M. COTE, JP MORGAN CHASE

I woke up one morning and realized that my democracy was missing! I looked in the closet, in the laundry hamper—maybe I left it in my jeans—I searched all over the house for it; even under my bed. I searched for hours. My democracy was forever lost. At first I panicked, but then quickly realized that I could swing by my congresswoman's office and pick up some more.

Later that morning, I put on my jeans, a clean shirt, along with my favorite pair of Nikes, and headed toward my congresswoman's office. As I approached her office, from a distance, I noticed a large black van parked in front. The van had one of those extended cabs. The license plate read "CHASE." As I neared her office, a procession of men, dressed in double breasted suits and carrying large bags over their shoulders, began walking from her office to the black van. The bags were labeled. The labels read "DEMOCRACY." I waited outside her office for the procession to end. Once the procession from the office had ended, I walked through the front office door and began walking up the stairs. On the stairs there were letters strewn about, some were broken and all had soiled footprints on them. There was an, Y, A, R, a couple of C's, I also saw a D, E, M, and O's.

Once at the top of the stairs, I noticed that my congresswoman's office door was open, so I walked in. With the exception of a solid oak desk, the room was completely void of any substance. The desk was stacked three feet high with cash. And at that moment, I realized that I didn't lose my democracy, it was taken from me.

Dave McGee

Citi

From a Former "Preferred Investor"

TO: WILLIAM S. THOMPSON JR., CITIGROUP

Hi Mr. Thompson!

My name's Thompson, too—who knows, maybe we're related in some distant way. Any relatives in North Carolina?

I know you're busy making poor decisions with people's life savings, so I'll keep this short and simple.

Five years ago I was a single, 49-year-old mom who owned her own home (I mean owned—paid off) and had a $175,000 IRA . . . with Citi. Not too shabby.

Today, I'm a single, 54-year-old mom who lost her home *and* her IRA in the process of trying to keep it. I got laid off two and a half years ago, and fortunately have found another job . . . with a foreign outsourced company making a fraction of what I used to make, no pension and lousy benefits.

I cannot only not afford to save, but I have had to eliminate the simple things I used to give my child, such as dance classes—her forte and her passion. Extraordinarily sad.

But hey, at least we're eating. Two years ago, I only ate dinner every other night. All I could afford.

I now look forward to literally another twenty-five years of full-time employment. I just hope my health holds out.

Enjoy your lovely home and your next vacation to the Seychelles. . . . Please remember me when you're there and send a postcard.

Sincerely,

Susan Thompson
North Carolina

Citigroup Education Loans

TO: JUDITH RODIN, CITIGROUP

Dear Ms. Rodin,

Thank you for taking the time out of your busy day to consider the story I have to tell. I am a 58-year-old single grandmother who teaches special education students in a California public school. I am proud of my career, my students, and my school. Our school is well known in our community as a school of character. As President of the Rockefeller Foundation, former president of University of Pennsylvania, and a current Citigroup board member, you, too, must value character.

In 2000 I was a married wife and mother of two fine sons. Our older son had recently graduated from a small private college and was fast making a name for himself in software research and development. My husband was a clergyman with a fair income, and I was happy to be paid the going rate as a public school teacher. Our second son had just been accepted to New York University. He, like his brother, was brilliant and talented, and had his heart set on NYU. We filled out the paperwork for financial aid, including applying for parent loans. Citi awarded us over $100,000 of parent loans during his college years.

But times change. My husband left. My older son battled medical problems that required him to return home. Costs of living increased without compensatory raises. Our home, which is every family's hedge against the future, had to be sold as debts grew. Sold in an upside-down housing market. But at least I could sell the house.

I now find myself owing nearly $100,000. Can I possibly work long enough to pay it off? I believe that the same banking policies that awarded home loans to people who were ultimately doomed to default also awarded parent and college loans far in excess of the borrowers' ability to repay.

When the Wall Street/banking crisis hit, the very corporations that had brought about the failure were "bailed out" by the citizens of this country. But when a single person unwisely burdened with too great a debt falls into crisis, there is nowhere to go. The safety net for individual citizens—bankruptcy—is unavailable to me. Not only do I "make too much," but education loans are not eradicated by bankruptcy or debt consolidation.

I am accustomed to making good decisions and paying my debts—to "making my own way." I believe Citigroup policies are in large measure responsible for the unbearable situation in which I now survive. I am not working to make a home or a future for myself. I am working to service my debt. As a woman of character, I beg you to consider your company's complicity in the unbearable situation in which I and millions of other American parents find ourselves. It is never too late for people of character to make a change.

With warmest regards,

Susan McGee
Rosemead, CA 91770

James Forese's $5 Million Citigroup Bonus after Losing $20 Billion

As a Citigroup client I was disturbed to read this: James Forese is a co-head of Citi's Institutional Client Group. This "Client Group" alone lost $20 billion in 2008. Yet Forese is rewarded a $5 million bonus (in 2009, 2010) under the Citigroup bonus plan after Citigroup got a staggering $250 billion bailout.*

* The letter writer is referring to _Time_ magazine's report on Citi's multi-million dollar plan for cash bonuses to executives in 2009. See Stephen Gandel, "Citigroup Plans Big Bonuses Despite Rules Against Them," _Time_, March 20, 2009.

It kills me that if I don't make a Citi credit card payment I am fucked! And that this asshole loses $20 billion, and gets a $5 million bonus for doing it!

Compensation

TO: VIKRAM S. PANDIT, CITIGROUP

Hi, Mr. Vikram Pandit.

I'm writing to discuss compensation packages at Citigroup. I've heard that you made $10,800,000 last year. Dude! That's awesome! I bet you can buy a lot of . . . stuff with that. Probably pretty cool stuff. To be honest, I'm not even sure what that much money can buy. I bet you get to fly business-class when you travel. Oh, or maybe you have a waterbed? I always wanted one of those. They seem to have fallen out of favor, for some reason. Do you have any idea why?

Anyway, I was wondering about the compensation for the bank tellers who work for you. I was thinking about how much work being a bank teller is, and it doesn't seem *that* hard, come to think of it. They're in an air-conditioned office, they (probably) have a chair. All things considered, it must be pretty cushy.

But then I remembered that you (I mean you, personally, your very own self, Mr. Vikram Pandit!) probably also have air conditioning and chairs and stuff (have you tried one of those Aeron chairs with the mesh back? *Divine*!). I mean, Mr. Pandit, you're not, you know, picking strawberries all day or anything. (I don't actually know how much money strawberry pickers make, but I have to assume it's *tons*; I mean, that's hard work!)

But even so, you're the boss and everything, so I'd guess that you might even work, say, 100 times as hard as your bank tellers.

So I was kind of wondering why your bank tellers don't make $108,000 a year, but instead have a base salary of less than $26,000? Have you been (accidentally, I'm sure) sending them the wrong paychecks? Or do you really think you work 415 times as hard as they do?

I mean, I'm sure your job must be very difficult, but do you really (like, really really?) think that you work 415 times as hard as your staff? Are you putting in 3,000 hour days or something? That would be pretty cool, but I'm not sure how that would work. Oh, wait! Maybe with all that money you bought a time-slower-thingy. I read about those in *Harry Potter*.

Anyway, I'd love to hear from you. Especially if you'd be willing to lend me your time machine. I've always wanted to see Europe during the feudal era. You're never going to believe this, but in that day and age (The Dark Ages!) there were kings and princes who didn't do anything to help the world and had so much money, and then peasants who had to toil all day in the fields for the royalty only to die miserable and poor and alone! Good grief, I'm glad we've come so far. Aren't you?

I hope you're having a great day! And wow, I hope it's less than 3,000 hours long! That would be *exhausting*!

Hugs and kisses,

Dave

THANKS FOR CARING

I FOOLISHLY TOOK OUT A PERSONAL LOAN TO PAY FOR A SEMESTER OF COLLEGE FROM CITI. NOW, I AM LAID OFF, BROKE, AND MY RETIRED PARENTS ON FIXED SOCIAL SECURITY ARE GETTING FIVE THREATENING PHONE CALLS A DAY FROM CITI. I HAVE NO WAY TO PAY, NEITHER DO THEY. NO FORBEARANCE LEFT. AND CITI GOT RID OF MY GRADUATED REPAYMENT OPTION. WTF MAN. NOT COOL. HOW BOUT SOME FLEXIBILITY AND LOWER MY REPAYMENT OPTIONS?

Trying Not to Go Under on Mortgage—Not Paying EZ Payment Fee

TO: VIKRAM S. PANDIT, CITIGROUP

Dear Mr. Pandit,

I want you to know that it took me over two-and-a-half years to get a rate modification on my current mortgage with Citigroup. It was such a tremendous hassle, it was incredible, but I went through with the process because I am desperately trying to keep my home.

I will say that after two and a half years of applications and hurdles, Citigroup did modify my mortgage rate. However you reneged on the original terms you quoted me. You quoted that my rate would be reduced from 6.5% to 3.2%, which would have been very helpful, but instead you reduced the rate to 4.5%. Big difference, but in any event, I accepted your graciousness. However, three months afterward, you increased my monthly payment by $500 because you felt I should add additional funds to my escrow account.

Unfortunately, this put a tremendous strain on me and, in my efforts to keep paying my mortgage on a timely basis, I tried to pay half the mortgage payment with every pay period, as I get paid every two weeks. I attempted to make half payments online but was unable to because the bank would only accept full monthly payment. I personally went to the bank and was told that I had to make the entire payment or instead enroll in an EZ Payment Program.

To join this incredible EZ Payment Program, which would allow me to make two payments a month, I must pay a $350 enrollment fee. Sounds like this is a bit inconsiderate, but since all I want to do is pay my mortgage on time, the best way I can pay on a timely basis is to join, but I cannot join unless I agree to pay the $350 fee. But of course, Citigroup cannot pass up yet another opportunity to generate another fee.

Because I did not agree to pay the $350 fee—which I can use to pay the dentist, or buy books for my son in college, or put food on my table, or pay off credit cards—I am behind on my mortgage and, in addition to the mortgage that I will have to wait to pay during my next pay period, I will be assessed a *late* fee, regardless if I try to pay you on time the best way I could.

I guess that no matter how you look at it, the bank never loses. They always win. And you wonder why the people are upset?

If the banks received government support to avoid bankruptcy, why can't you pay this forward and help those who need help as well?

Please know that regardless, I refuse to pay the $350 fee to enroll in your EZ Payment Program. I do not care if I go under, but I will *not* pay it. This is flagrant *greed, greed, greed*. When will you stop this flagrant *greed*?

Citibank Fraud

TO: MANUEL MEDINA-MORA, CITIGROUP

Your company admitted to fraud recently. Agreed to fork over hundreds of millions to say sorry. How do you feel about working for such a company?

Why I'm Leaving Citibank after Nearly Twenty Years

Hello,

I'm sure you've heard a lot of news about the whole OWS movement. I wanted you to personally know why I, this one random person in California, would leave the bank I've been with for twenty years. I'm not a big depositor, so you probably don't care about just me. But what if tens of thousands like me do the same—then will you care?

I grew up professionally working in banking. I worked at the Federal Reserve for five years. I am a capitalist and I believe in the banking system.

But what Citibank, B of A, Chase, Goldman Sachs and many others are doing to this country is . . . well, "disheartening" is putting it mildly.

What if Citibank acknowledged this and found a way to support OWS—wouldn't that set you apart from your competitors?! I know—not likely, but hopefully Citibank will see what's happening and not respond with the same arrogance as B of A. If so, I'll leave my new credit union and happily come back to Citibank.

Thanks for listening.

Words of Encouragement from a Long-Time Fan

TO: PETER ORSZAG, CITIGROUP

When you joined the Obama executive team with what appeared to be a knowledgeable and progressive background, I was thrilled. *Finally*, I thought, *here's someone who understands the plight of labor, who can listen with an open mind to the concerns of those at the mercy of economic vicissitudes.* I had a great deal of hope. I thought change would be possible.*

---

* Peter Orszag was Special Assistant to the President for Economic Policy and a Senior Economist and Senior Adviser on the Council of Economic Advisers during the Clinton administration. He became Obama's Director of the Office of Management and Budget from 2008 to 2010.

Surely now, from the executive board of Citigroup, you continue your selfless service to the American populace—unencumbered by the demands of democracy and transparency, the generous compensation package merely bolstering your dedication to the cause.

No doubt we can expect broad increases in prosperity, a rising tide lifting boats across all income groups, as a result of your work at Citigroup. The prevailing trend toward inequality will be dramatically reversed any day now.

What a fine leader you turned out to be. The American people certainly deserve nothing less.

Kate

Unable to Refinance

I bought my home in 2002 and over the years my mortgage ended up with Citibank. This letter is addressed to them.

I have never missed a payment, and I have not lost my job, and I have no credit card debt. However, because of the economy, my $100,000 house is now worth an estimated $27,000. I still owe $70,000. I tried to refinance. Tried to get the lower rates that are out there. But instead of trying to help me, you wouldn't because the house wouldn't approve for what I still owe on it.

Initially, I didn't understand why you wouldn't work with people?! I have no signs of being a high risk. In fact, you jerks pre-approved me for a second mortgage (that I did not end up taking!). How come I can get pre-approved for another $100,000, but I'm not eligible to refinance? I'll tell you why. You don't make as much money if my payments go down! But oh, you'd just love to give me a second mortgage to make me pay even more interest!

Maybe if you helped people who want to continue paying and aren't at fault for the new assessed value of their home, people wouldn't hate you so much.

Goldman Sachs

An Open Letter to Goldman Sachs CEO Lloyd Blankfein

TO: LLOYD C. BLANKFEIN, GOLDMAN SACHS

Mr. Blankfein,

So, I've been writing these letters to bank CEOs where I gently rib them about stuff like "being abysmally terrible at their jobs" and "openly stealing from the general populace" and "having the morality of a supervillain" and stuff like that. You know. The usual. And so I was writing one to you about what a terrible businessman you are, and how you had to get your old boss to give you $64 billion because of how badly you suck at being a CEO. Ha, ha. It was going to be funny.

So I was doing research to find more things to make fun of you about. But I kept reading more and more about what a hive of scum and villainy your company actually is, and the more I read the less I felt like being funny. Because, you know, whatever. Any jackass can illegally accept naked short sales or underwrite bonds *and* encourage people to short those bonds or help Greece hide the true nature of its debt in order to make some extra cash, causing long-term damage to not just Greece but the whole Eurozone and therefore the world economy—which is at risk of going under (again!) partially because of your nefarious deeds (again! I guess you *can* fool people twice!). Hell, I could do that.

But really it was in finding out that your company's creation of the Goldman Sachs Commodity Index helped literally starve millions of people that I stopped feeling jokey and started actually feeling pity for you.* That's the worst thing to feel for somebody, Lloyd, because it means I consider you less than me. You know what? I do!

I'm asking this honestly: How do you sleep at night? I know that sounds all melodramatic, but when I've, you know, inadvertently hurt somebody's *feelings*, I have trouble getting any rest at all. I can't imagine ever getting a bit of shut-eye again if I found out I helped artificially drive up the price of wheat in the greatest year of plenty the world had ever known, pushing 250,000,000 more people to the breaking point and causing food riots in thirty countries.

You must either have a really comfortable bed or a metric boatload of Ambien. Or no conscience whatsoever, and such broken morality that you don't realize what damage your little money games are causing the planet.

No, I'm just playing, I'm sure you're a great guy. Ha, ha.

Dave
New York, NY 10039

* See Frederick Kaufman, "The Food Bubble: How Wall Street Starved Millions and Got Away with It," <u>Harper's</u>, July 2010.

$9,165 an hour—Wow Lloyd, You're a Big Earner

TO: LLOYD C. BLANKFEIN, GOLDMAN SACHS

Hi Lloyd,

So I just read online that your salary in 2010—including all of those delightful perks that just put a smile on one's face—is $19.06 million.

And your hourly wage is $9,165. That's great! Do you even collect that much when you take lunch?

Do you realize that by working a mere two hours you earn as much as someone who works full-time at minimum wage earns in a year?

Wondering if I could have your job for say, three hours a week. Would that be too much to ask?

You can leave the stuff that you don't like about your job to me: talking to the press about Occupy Wall Street, testifying at hearings about board members who are charged with insider trading. You know, all that icky stuff.

You can still wheel-and-deal and be your macho master-of-the-universe self. I'll just do the three hours of grunt work you don't like each week.

What do you say, Lloyd? Deal?

Susie
Meriden, CT

Hello Edith—Wow, Now I Know a 1 Percenter!

TO: EDITH W. COOPER, GOLDMAN SACHS

Greetings Edith,

I hope this message finds you well. Gosh, I am thrilled to meet you, even though we haven't met face-to-face . . . yet!

I mean, *wow*, I actually *know* a 1 percenter now! How cool is this?

Of course, you probably don't have much to worry about even if you're not feeling well, because I trust that you have great health insurance—thanks to me helping pay for it.

Wow, Edith, how great is that! :)

Since I hope we get to know one another better, here's a little bit of info about me: I have a degree in journalism and my hubby has a double Master's in music, but since we're over 50 years old, our premiums climbed, so we were faced with a slippery slope choice . . . Do we eat, or do we pay for health insurance? It was a toss-up, but we decided that food was more important.

Oh wait—you haven't heard about our foreclosure! Law enforcement came to our door and gave us *one hour* to vacate! Oh, that morning was so much fun—I wish you could have been there! Yes, we were in that first wave in '08, after putting down a down payment of . . . wait for it . . . $300,000.

We totally qualified, you see . . . hubby had a great business, until his clients could no longer pay him

. . . Our lender told us "don't worry, we want to work with you! We can see you have never been in trouble before!"—and well, it's a long story.

I'll save the rest of this story for next time, because I am so looking forward to writing back again . . . very, very soon.

Your new pen pal,

Hilary Grant
Los Osos, CA 93402

P.S. I can't wait to hear about the beautiful clothes you must wear. I buy all of my clothes these days at thrift stores, but maybe we can compare notes?

An Opportunity

TO: LLOYD C. BLANKFEIN, GOLDMAN SACHS

Dear Mr. Blankfein,

We are writing to you to interest you in a fantastic new opportunity for you and your loved ones. We are offering you the once in a lifetime opportunity to refinance all of your many homes and/or jets for the wealth—oops, did I say *wealth*—equity that you are holding in them.

Did you know that the property you bought for millions is actually worth gazillions of dollars under this plan? Yes! Gazillions! With our excellent and trustworthy panel of advisors we can help you truly capitalize on your investments and really make the most of what life has to offer.

What we do is: take the money you "earned" during those fantastic boom years, and invest it in schools, hospitals, housing and jobs for the poor, educate feed and clothe people before their brief yet worthy lives extinguish.

There really is nothing to lose from your side: just take the money backed by the assets of the houses, jets, boats and jewelry, sign your name, and we can provide you with short-term aspirations! It really is that simple. And don't take our word for it, talk to many of our other customers in the 1% base range. Plenty of satisfaction all round!

With Such Sincerely Tepid Regards,

OWS Refinancing

Eternally Indebted

TO: ABBY JOSEPH COHEN, GOLDMAN SACHS

Hello,

My name is Mike Eastwood, I'm just a 20-year-old kid from a small town in Oklahoma, but let me tell you my story. I come from a stable and mostly happy family life. I have two sisters (I'm a middle child) who graduated valedictorians of their high schools. I graduated with a 3.7 GPA from my 3A high school in 2009.

My older sister graduated in 2003 from a state college. She worked for the next five years but has been inconsistently employed and predominantly unemployed since 2008, when she moved to San Diego to join her husband who was stationed there by the Marines. All the while, she's been trying to pay off the $90,000 in student loans she racked up while trying to get a degree in pharmaceuticals that she is not able to use.

I am still going through college, attempting a degree in history. I decided to go to a community college after high school to avoid debt. I've been attending classes that do not challenge me intellectually in any way because, frankly, I was and am too scared of the debt that comes from a decent school. I do this in hopes that I can someday be a teacher, though I know that is a career that will leave me in debt for the rest of my life, regardless of how hard I work. My younger sister just graduated (again, a valedictorian with a 4.0 GPA) and she chose not to go to college after seeing the debt involved in getting a degree, as well as numerous examples of people racking up debt for a degree that doesn't help them move forward in life. Each of us attempted and qualified for many scholarships but none of us qualified for PELL Grants or FAFSA Student Aid. Our parents combined (my mother is a teacher, my father runs a collating machine) make about $65,000 a year, putting us just out of reach of any federal assistance.

Why do I mention this to you? Goldman Sachs doesn't have anything to do with school directly and I can't place the blame for our debts on the shoulders of your corporation, nor would I try to. I tell you this because I want to show the state and cost of education, even at a local level, and far more importantly, I want to bring to your awareness the lives of those people who seem to have slipped beyond the vision of you and your fellow executives. My sister, with $90,000 in total student loans and paying a bit above the minimum payment (minimum payment is $345 a month; she pays $400) and paying against an 8.9% annual interest rate, cannot successfully pay off that student loan during her lifetime, assuming she is forced to continue working for K-Mart. And to perhaps offer a bit more perspective on her situation, she works forty hours a week at the minimum wage of $7.25, which earns her roughly $780 a month. Just repaying her student loans costs her more than half of her total income and it's a payment that will never end.

Again, this isn't your fault. She didn't make the job market for those entering the field of pharmaceuticals plummet. And again, I do not blame Goldman Sachs for these problems. Allow me to give another example. As I said before, I'm only 20 years old. I was diagnosed with juvenile diabetes in April of this year. Type-1 diabetes means I'll have to take insulin shots for the rest of my life, avoid some foods, and remove other foods from my diet completely. I was diagnosed after attending a local soccer game where I fell unconscious while sitting and watching. My blood sugar had gotten so high that the fact I hadn't had a stroke was a true miracle (1,115, in case you're curious.) This serious medical problem and diagnosis cost me $2,470. I will also have to pay nearly $160 a month for all of my insulin and diabetes supplies. I don't have health care myself, but fortunately, because I'm under 24 and thanks to the new laws passed in 2010, I can remain listed on my mother's health insurance.

Unfortunately, my mother is a teacher and her coverage is not all that great. On top of my now $15,000 in school debt and the $1,045 loan I took out last January to cover the cost of my and my fiancé's bills for a month when she was out of work, I'm in a lot of debt for a kid who was only in high school two years ago, and it is especially high considering that I live in a one-bedroom apartment with my fiancé, I drive a beat-up 1994 Pontiac Sunbird, and try desperately not to exceed my means.

I want to stress that I don't blame Goldman Sachs for these problems; I'm not trying to insinuate in any way that you are at fault for this debt or these problems in my life or my family's lives. What I do want to show you is the gap between the lives of everyday Americans and the lives you all lead as the executives of such a prestigious operation. Between your lives and the lives of those of us who have had to struggle and fight for every bit of happiness we have.

You've influenced our government elections using more than $11,200,000 for the sake of your own interests, leaving the American people with no other alternative but to watch and pray it all gets better. Your profits in 2010 were about $21,700,000,000. My siblings and I made a combined $31,859 and, with my parents' income, that's $96,859. This is barely enough to pay back my older sister's student loans. My family, with the possible exception of my father, is well-educated, hardworking, and politically involved, and yet there is no light at the end of the tunnel. "Work hard and you'll have a good life" is a cruel axiom.

The reason I send you this message is so that you might read it and understand that we are frustrated by our lives, by the fact that a huge portion of our incomes are taken away for the sake of supporting federal and state governments that ignore the people they are supposed to represent, and that ignore them because global business juggernauts have the ability to simply buy a vote. Your corporate tax breaks are ridiculous. Your unlimited access to involvement in the affairs of the politics that are supposed to allow the people to improve the quality of their own lives is cruel and unfair. Most of all, your ignorance of the trials and hardships of the average American is unforgivable.

Please understand why we stand in the streets with signs. It is not for handouts, it's not to taunt or torment the rich, and it's most certainly not because a bunch of lazy, uneducated hippies want to lay blame on the shoulders of giant corporations. It's because our lives are in shambles and because you have taken from us our only outlet for change. So we forge a new outlet and we stand shoulder to shoulder in solidarity. Let us change, begin to change yourselves, so that we will again have the American Dream.

Michael Eastwood
Bartlesville, Oklahoma 74003

Understanding Capitalism

TO: SARAH G. SMITH, GOLDMAN SACHS

I really cannot believe that none of you bourgeoisie understand the system you advocate. You do understand that the free market is against government intervention? You do understand that bailouts *are* government intervention? Does this fact go over your head? Do you lie to yourself every day to cover this fact up?

I'll try and help you with some good criticism: Practice what you preach and reject my tax dollars. You want the free market, then accept it. You failed and failed huge, so you should fail. Sure, you'd lose money but you'd be truthful. You would have a clear conscience and could sleep at night.

I'm reminded of a quote from Lenin, though, that helps me understand everything: Capitalists are no more capable of self-sacrifice than a man is capable of lifting himself up by his own bootstraps. I would love to see a part of the 1% pull themselves up physically by their own bootstraps.

Hey Lloyd!

TO: LLOYD C. BLANKFEIN, GOLDMAN SACHS

I work in financial services, and I understand that you've had a tough past few years. Why not retire? You have plenty of money and millions of people hate your guts.

What I don't get is that Goldman, under your leadership, essentially became insolvent, and because of a bailout from our government, the firm continues to exist. Granted, I was for the bailout, and I'm happy that you paid it all back. The part that I am confused about is why you're still there. I've been a shareholder in Goldman, and the way I see it, if the person driving my car puts it into a ditch and needs a tow, that person shouldn't drive the car anymore. But that's neither here nor there.

I am looking out for you. Our business is a miserable one. Most of it (except for you because you are the boss) is sitting in front of an Excel worksheet for ten to eighteen hours a day thinking about what life would be if you weren't wasting away. You aren't old, but you aren't young either. Maybe you should enjoy some of life. When you are on your deathbed, you will wish that you'd spent some time with your family or went on that trip that you'd always wanted to take or whatnot. Perhaps you could become an advocate of the 99%. I doubt you would, but Buffett (the guy who saved your ass) did. History would look more favorably on you at least. Life is short, you can't buy time, and you have plenty of money to enjoy the rest of yours.

If you ever want to talk, just reply to this message and I'll send you my phone info. Have a good night.

Ian Gaida
Brooklyn, NY 11211

Congrats on a Job Well Done

TO: LLOYD C. BLANKFEIN, GOLDMAN SACHS

I was just wondering if you could fill me in on how to not get fired when you're horrible at your job? I saw some people got to "resign" and then were rewarded with million-dollar contracts. That seems pretty cool. And how to avoid being indicted when you obviously broke the law? It's the least you can do for the people seeing as how America bailed you out. Does playing dumb really work? Because it seems like it did in your case . . .

If you really felt bad about what happened, you should have cut bonuses and offered up some of your money when shit hit the fan. But instead you rewarded yourself some more. So I guess the bonus was really for just showing up.

I hope the saying "cheaters never prosper" turns true in your case. A good starting point for you would be to stop stealing, stop cheating, and get your corporate money out of politics. I would like to see the Justice Department bring charges. Seems like a matter that is worth my time so hopefully I can help push that along.

We Are Hurting

TO: JOHN S. WEINBERG, GOLDMAN SACHS

Dear Mr. Weinberg,

I write to you from Manhattan, where I live thanks to rent control. Without rent control, my fiancé and I would be forced to live far from where we work and study here in the city. I am a full-time graduate student working on my PhD in History and I am a state-employed teaching assistant at Stony Brook University, SUNY, on Long Island. It's a long commute, but I can't complain.

You'd think that someone pursuing a PhD and teaching college courses at a university would not have anything to complain about in this economy. You'd think that there must be a big difference between me and the folks protesting at Occupy Wall Street. You're wrong.

To teach college students about American history, New York state only pays me about $15,000. My fiancé, also a PhD student, is not offered any sort of employment from her university. Thus we live in Manhattan on $15,000 a year. After taxes, health care costs, and student fees, we actually live on about $10,000 a year. Did you know that for a household of two, making $10,000 a year puts you under the federal poverty line? That's right, two PhD students in Manhattan live in poverty. But why is this so?

Most of my grievances are against SUNY and against my elected representatives at the state and federal levels. But I am also mad at Wall Street. Because Goldman Sachs along with other banks were bailed out by the US government after they made stupid and reckless financial decisions in 2007. But were we ever bailed out?

You probably get a very nice salary, and perhaps even bonuses. How many times higher is your salary than mine? And tell me, is the reason you get paid so much, and is the reason you get bonuses, because you have been so successful in foreclosing on working people's homes? Or is it because you've been so successful in funding the political parties or candidates that will "protect" you from regulation and shield you from paying a fair share of taxes? What are you doing that earns you such high pay that is somehow more valued than all my efforts to teach the next generation of college students?

All I'm asking is: fire all the top employees at your company who were responsible for bringing on the economic recession. And don't give them severance bonuses. Stop putting all your corporate money into state and federal politics. Support laws restricting the amount of money corporations can donate to political parties and PACs. Support a constitutional amendment that will make clear that corporations are not to be considered "people" under US law. Support increased taxes on the top 1% of wealthiest Americans and on corporations.

Thank you for your time and consideration. I look forward to your response.

Sincerely,

Gregory Rosenthal

From a Stockholder of Your Company

TO: GARY D. COHN, GOLDMAN SACHS

Hello Mr. Cohn,

I was given stock as a gift from my hardworking, railroad-employed grandfather a few years ago.

Several years ago, as a way to diversify this stock, my advisor at Smith Barney suggested I place some of my money in Goldman Sachs.

Because your company uses practices that both alienate the 99% of the people who, like me, could never afford stocks on our own and that benefit the wealthy and powerful, I am asking that your company practice ethical procedures. This includes keeping shareholder money, including my own, out of the political system of the US. Without this change, it will be difficult for me to remain a shareholder who, because of your company's decisions, participates in such unethical procedures.

My Story

TO: GREGORY K. PALM, GOLDMAN SACHS

Just before my daughter graduated from high school in 2008, she had a healthy college fund. It was not a huge fund, but we had worked hard and set aside enough to pay for her tuition and some of her living expenses. She chose a prestigious school out of state and received a

Presidential Merit scholarship. Her hope was that she could concentrate on her undergraduate education, make the most of her studies, and rocket via scholarship into graduate school and be on her way to a successful career. The story didn't go that way.

As the stock market crashed, so did her nest egg. She's had to work two part-time jobs to pay her living expenses in order to save her college fund for tuition. In addition, every year she is borrowing the maximum amount of student loan that is available to her. The result? She still can't afford to pay for her senior year of college. She is considering transferring to a local college in order to graduate. So long, prestigious school diploma. On the day that she graduates, she will be $30,000 in debt.

At the same time that tuition expenses gobbled up what was left of our daughter's college fund, banks were bailing each other out and helping themselves to federal tax dollars like it was a land rush. As each semester passes and she goes further into debt, top bank executives give themselves another million-dollar bonus. Unfortunately, here at home, we can't help her out because our own savings have dwindled. Our home is not worth what we owe for it, so we can't even reduce our expenses. Our situation is not unusual. It is the situation of the majority of Americans.

You did this to American citizens. You did this. You need to fix it.

Tired of Elites Working in Wall Street

TO: GREGORY K. PALM, GOLDMAN SACHS

Hi,

I, too, once worked briefly on Wall Street, and what I witnessed was extremely sad. So many of the brightest science and math graduates from the finest universities have passed on a life of cutting-edge research and developing technological solutions to better society in favor of pointless days trading on financial exchanges. These are the same folks who have developed CDOs, CDSs, and all kinds of other useless arcane derivatives. None of this creates any wealth or value for the 99%.

I'm sick and tired of the nonstop lobbying for greater deregulation, sick and tired of billionaire hedge fund managers having the lowest tax rates, and just plain sick and tired of the short-term thinking that has come to dominate the culture. I am happy to see that your company lost revenue and plans to sack more financiers and hustlers at your corporation. I will boycott Goldman Sachs and I will do what I can to prevent companies like yours from recruiting on campuses.

Jason Novotny
Berkeley, CA 94703

Nice to Meet You!

TO: SARAH G. SMITH, GOLDMAN SACHS

Dear Sarah,

I'm looking forward to being your pen pal! Let me tell you a little about myself and my family. I live in Denver, CO and work for a nonprofit that helps crime victims. I've been doing this for about ten years professionally, fifteen years if you count my prior volunteer experience. I make just shy of $50,000 a year and pay around 30% of my income in taxes.

My sweetheart, who I will be marrying in April, is a temporary employee of the Postal Service. Did you know that the USPS doesn't even hire full-time, benefited employees anymore? He went to school to be an electrician, but he graduated in 2008. You remember what was going on in 2008, dontcha? I'm sure you were pretty focused on your own company's woes, but in our world, that was also the first time in fifty years that the electricians' union wasn't taking on new apprentices. Wages have since fallen around 50% for apprentice electricians and my sweetie took the USPS job with no benefits and no security because he couldn't afford to make $11/hour. He also pays around 30% in taxes. We hope to be able to buy a home and have a baby in the next few years. We're both in our thirties and the proverbial biological clock is ticking away, but I'd be lying if I said we don't stress about how to pull it off every single day.

Sarah, I will be writing you again and I want you to know that I will never send you mean, nasty messages just because you work for Goldman Sachs or because I know that your life circumstances look a helluva lot different than mine. I am just hopeful that you will read my letters and think about your own life and what you contribute to our country. I'd like you to think about how much you make, how much you donate and how much you pay in taxes. Now, please don't let that voice in your head say, *But, I'm a job creator*! I didn't mention that I am an assistant director of my program and have employees of my own, not to mention crime victims, that I am responsible for. I am a huge fan of the late Paul Wellstone and he had a saying: "We all do better when we all do better." I hope you will think about that and remember that you, as a badass female executive, could be such an agent of change for future generations.

I will write again soon. I hope you have a nice week.

Sincerely,

Sterling Marie
Denver, CO 80223

Please Blow That Whistle

TO: EDITH W. COOPER, GOLDMAN SACHS

Hi Edith,

I'm probably old enough to be your mother. I am alarmed at the enormous profits you and your colleagues are making at my expense—not to mention the burden it will put on my daughter and granddaughters. Much of my savings have gone to bail out your colleagues (maybe you, too). A way was found to "share the risk," but not the gains, among all of us suckers. Please, we count on you to have the courage to blow the whistle. You know what's right. Please do it.

Thank you from the bottom of my heart for having the courage to act now.

Judy Reichler
New Paltz, NY 12561

You've Come a Long Way from Yankee Stadium

TO: LLOYD C. BLANKFEIN, GOLDMAN SACHS

Dear Lloyd (may I call you Lloyd?),

I really like this idea of those of us in the 99% reaching out in understanding to those of you on Wall Street who are currently getting such a spotlight on your adventures. But the more I look, the less I understand. In fact, I've written to another Wall Streeter who also surprised me when I read up on her background.

I know you and Goldman have gotten a lot of heat lately and I assumed you were some privileged, out-of-touch, always-been-rich person who just didn't get how tough it is to be a working-class stiff in a society that no longer manufactures anything. But Lloyd, you worked selling hot dogs and Cracker Jacks at Yankee Stadium! You went through the NYC public school system! Your parents were the same type of working stiffs who are losing their homes, jobs, and savings thanks to the policies of our bought-out government. If I read your background up until you get to go to Harvard instead of Brooklyn College, you sound like all my friends.

I picked you as Goldman's head to write to because of the revolving door between the federal government and your company. But now I really have to ask the same question that I've seen asked by others here. How do you sleep at night? When is enough enough? You'd already reached the pinnacle of success, so why does it seem that you and those others like you were so willing to push Wall Street to the extremes that culminated in the financial crises?

I'm sure everyone you knew growing up understood what it was like to be concerned about getting a decent job, having a decent place to live, and supporting a family. So when you think about the people protesting the excesses and greed of the banks and financial institutions, maybe you want to remember where you came from.

Public Education

TO: LLOYD C. BLANKFEIN, GOLDMAN SACHS

Dear Mr. Blankfein,

I am a public school teacher in Allendale, New Jersey. While Goldman Sachs accepted a $10 billion bailout, thousands of public school employees in NYC alone lost their jobs, and class sizes skyrocketed. How can we educate the employees of tomorrow if we do not have the proper staffing or resources to do so? Do you remember how many students were in each class when you went to school?

Open Letter to Mr. Blankfein

TO: LLOYD C. BLANKFEIN, GOLDMAN SACHS

Mr. Blankfein:

First off, I would like to say congratulations. While you are doing "God's Work" up there at Goldman Sachs, I'm up at 1:14 AM trying to figure out how I'm going to make ends meet when the night turns into morning. I can hear my father in the room next to mine stirring as well.

You see, your bank had this Private Equity fund, which bought his company, saddled it with debt, and then quickly drove it into bankruptcy. You then flipped it for a very large profit, and left a shell of a company that is now struggling day to day under an incredible debt load (all for having the privilege of buying itself). Now my father's thirty years of hard work is being rewarded by you fellows sacking his pension, selling his years of accumulated bonus stocks (on his behalf and in his best interest at 41 cents a share during bankruptcy proceedings, even though his cost was $40 a share and said shares were part of his retirement plan)—and who knows what tomorrow will bring. I can't help but tear up to think about his friends at work, twenty-five, thirty, even forty years of devoted service to a company that is probably going to turn around and reward them with a pink slip tomorrow. It's a shame: all in the name of profit, they tell us.

Yet his only concern is us, his children. Bravery comes in many shapes and sizes, and can be found in many places. When I think of people to look up to and admire, I don't look to Wall Street and people like you. I look to Main Street, and I hope my generation and future generations can exhibit half the bravery and honesty that our middle-aged and middle-class forefathers have shown during these tough times.

That isn't the worst of it, for us anyways. How about my sister and I, just about to turn 27 and 30 respectively? We both have Master's degrees and loads of experience. Turns out that has not been enough for us either, as we both have lost our jobs during the credit crisis of 2007, and our dignity as well (and now live with our parents, which as you can imagine, was not a big part of our lifelong goals). I would like to get on with my life, you see, sir, as I've done my seven years of school, my five years of work, and many, many hours of volunteer work. I have done my time and paid my experiential dues. I would like to get back to being a good upstanding citizen and contributor to the tax base in my country, and to getting my student loans settled, just as my fellow family members and friends across America would like to do. Heck, I pray nightly for a job at a respectable place such as the local 7-Eleven. After a year of searching for work, it would be nice to know that my seven days a week of pounding the pavement will have paid off, and I can at least settle my debts, pay my bills, and cut my losses with dignity. Yet the actions of Wall Street, Bay Street, and *the* Street make this completely impossible for us.

But here is the best part, the kicker (if you will). I'm not from the United States. We don't live anywhere near you hotshots in New York City. Yet your team members, doing "God's Work" have vastly affected lives not only in the United States, but in fact all over the world. You and your fellow compadres will have to pay for that someday, so I'd start making a game plan of restitution to society really soon. I mean, metaphorically, the lone jailbird (I suppose that would be you) trying to escape the prison could very well get away; my money remains on the warden.

If we have learned anything in this crisis, it's that borders are only imaginary and people can only be restrained for so long. The whole world is uprising. But that doesn't mean it is too late for you to join us. We really could use some ideas from incredibly smart people such as yourself on how to fix the problems we currently *all* have (and not just fixes that work in your best interest). After all, you and your friends supposedly even have the big guy's attention (you even work for him!), and we could really use all the help we can get. Why not join us, the 99%? That way we can all constructively create a system where everyone prospers, including yourselves. That way we can get back to our lives, and you and your friends can get back to doing your jobs and making the big guy happy. Man, you can't ask for better PR than that!

In conclusion, I hope you have a wonderful day at work (yes, I'm jealous, I wish I had a job, too) and please do not hesitate to come downstairs at some point. I'm sure the people in New York City would love to have you join them.

I also would like to wish you good health, prosperity, and the same to all the fellow Americans who are struggling with us. It will get better, friends. We have their attention, thanks to your brave actions.

Much Love,

M. Scott
Canada

Retired Grandma

TO: SARAH G. SMITH, GOLDMAN SACHS

Hi Sarah,

By way of introduction, I'm a 63-year-old retired grandma living in central California. Hope you are doing well and having a great Saturday, because I am. Even living on $1,114-a-month social security income, I have a good life. Now this may indicate to you that I am stupid and slothful—not true.

When the 2008 financial debacle and subsequent TARP funds were approved by Congress to help you out, I thought, *Hmm, this doesn't smell right.* Being retired, I have a lot of free time to do research into what caused this collapse and Goldman Sachs' contribution to it. I must say, Goldman Sachs is impressive! And, of course, your good buddy Hank Paulson came through like a champ! What a guy! Tell him "Hi" from me, won't you? Tim Geithner was a bit of a rube, but he's still up in DC helping out and he's learned a lot, don't you think?

And the whole unregulated derivative market? Best thing *ever*! You guys are *so* clever, no wonder you are paid like kings, worth every penny and then some.

But I have to tell you, Sarah, I'm starting to become concerned for your welfare. Thanks to the internet, word spread pretty darned fast about just how this happened, and of course there's online streaming videos and YouTube, so we don't rely on the mainstream media for information. Remember, "He who controls the message, controls the dialogue"? Not so much anymore and that's why I'm really concerned about you and your colleagues. See, we 99% don't rely on CBS, FOX, NBC, or ABC for "news" anymore. Why would we? Its laughable, fall-down-funny incompetence isn't worth our time. And I agree 100% in GS' corporate mandate—life is a meritocracy and if you can't stand the heat, get out of the kitchen (actually, my Mom used to say that last part). But, you get my drift.

Anyway, please let me know how you're doing and I look forward to hearing from you real soon.

Best regards.

What Happened to Your Integrity and Honor?

I worked for Goldman Sachs when I was 17 years of age. America had the politically disenfranchised in 1967, but economically the wealth of this country was far more equitable. The letter as well as spirit of the law that made that golden age possible has been dismantled over the past fifty years by those who work for you, doing your bidding. It seems that thieving and calling it the entrepreneurial spirit has become the rule, and all of America has greatly suffered for it.

You insist on lining your pockets at the expense of the common good. You believe you're entitled; that you deserve to be the exception; that you are the fittest—but all you really are is the worst type of parasite. So if the feeling that motivates you more than the greed is fear, it's time you detoxed from your addiction, as it is destroying what has made this country great.

Anthony Martin Dambrosi
Middletown, NY 10940

Did You Give Any More Consideration to My Proposal?

TO: LLOYD C. BLANKFEIN, GOLDMAN SACHS

Dear Lloyd,

I hope you had a great weekend and are planning for a really fun Halloween.

I was just wondering if you've given any more thought to my proposal . . . where you let me do your job for just three hours a week. As I noted in my last letter to you, your hourly wage is over $9,000. If I can just have three hours a week (really, how much would you notice?) for one year, well, that would set me up for life.

The Trouble is the Banks

And when I say set me up for life, I truly mean it. You see, I'm 50. The first thirteen years of my career were with MCI, and I lost everything in that company's bankruptcy. And then I kept getting laid off for one reason or another. My jobs since MCI:

Interworld—an Internet start-up that went bust because the CEO was too busy playing with the polo team he'd purchased.

Marsh, Inc.—laid off when the whole March/AIG price-fixing scandal broke, the Marsh stock tanked, and massive layoffs resulted.

Since then I've been freelancing, and it's been alright. I started an SEP, but well, you know what happened in 2008.

But you see, my expenses aren't that high. So I really mean it when I say that having just three hours a week of your employment for one year would really set me up for life.

Please respond. You're the best!

Susie
Meriden, CT

Wells Fargo

My Experience

We, the 99%, are angry because all the financial breaks have gone to the CEOs and the big banks. We, when we encountered financial difficulty, did not get a bailout. Laws were passed in the last decade with intense lobbying by the banks so that we, when faced with unanticipated financial emergency or distress, could not declare bankruptcy with personal home mortgages and get help to keep our homes with reduced principal and interest.

And yet, people with second and third homes can get relief—big companies and banks can and do get relief, as we recently watched with TARP. Big corporations routinely file for bankruptcy and start afresh.

I am now 64 and a retired public school teacher; I lost my house last year. I still am almost incredulous that this happened to me: a middle class, well-educated woman. Yes, the loan was a predatory loan with a hefty pre-payment penalty the first two years. When my house was taken by Wells Fargo, I had invested hundreds of thousands of dollars in this house (from my monthly teacher paycheck). So much money—gone. And now my home is gone.

The servicing company (under Wells Fargo) was so inept, my head spun. The foreclosure process was so stressful that I developed serious anxiety for the very first time in my life. It will be doubly hard, at my age and stage in life, to rebuild my life and own my own home again. And I loved owning my own home. It's the American dream for a good reason.

Everyone deserves a fresh start sometimes, not just big business. We are fed up with the inequity, and wonder why the 1% in general don't seem to realize that a healthy middle class in America is what will keep us great, not hoarding most of the wealth and letting the rest suffer and sink. We will not be silent anymore.

Barbara Hall
Avery, CA 95370

Loan Modification

TO: JOHN G. STUMPF, WELLS FARGO

Dear John G. Stumpf,

I received a Loan Modification offered by Wells Fargo on October 28, 2010. These programs offer different options for borrowers in different situations, but all are meant to help people keep their homes when facing a significant hardship.

I was very grateful for this loan modification in my time of hardship. However, it was never divulged that if I accepted this loan modification my credit would be *ruined*! I was specifically told that this loan modification was to help me in a time of need. This hit to my credit score will take me ten years or more to fix. A good credit score is a necessity in these times! After completing the loan modification program I promptly paid my loan in full and will never use Wells Fargo again!

I wrote a letter to the credit dispute department asking Wells Fargo to fix this problem with my credit. On September 27, 2011 I got a letter in response stating that there was nothing that could be done. I am *enraged* at Wells Fargo for ruining my credit score! I thought Wells Fargo was offering me help in my time of need, but instead they destroyed my credit and made it almost impossible to receive any credit for many years! I *need* this problem fixed! My voice will be heard!

I Withdrew All My Money Today from Wells Fargo

I'm moving to a credit union where I know my money will be handled in accordance with my values, not used to further bankrupt the 99%.

Longtime Customer

TO: JOHN G. STUMPF, WELLS FARGO

Dear John,

I would like you to know that I have been a Wells Fargo customer for over ten years now. In that ten years, I have had years where I earned over six figures and years where I earned barely enough to pass the poverty level. I have banked with you through it all.

However, I have noticed that banking fees and requirements on my accounts have become more stringent, expensive, and extensive over the years. The most recent example of this was when I received the notification that, to avoid monthly fees, I would need to open another account, since my checking and savings accounts were not enough. This seemed to come just after the notification that I needed to have at least two accounts to avoid fees. Now, I hear that Wells Fargo is experimenting with monthly fees for debit card use. I am so disappointed in this current trend, which Wells Fargo increasingly uses to take advantage of the people it already does business with.

I hope that you are taking the Occupy Wall Street movements happening around the country and world very seriously. To think that only "slackers," "pot heads," and "flash mobs" are participating, or that the movement has more to do with general despair due to economic conditions, is simply wrong.

I strongly support this movement. I am neither a college student nor described by any of the names listed above. I am a graduate-school-educated financial industry professional. I, like millions of others in the US alone, am feeling firsthand the erosion of the middle class.

Ignore or dismiss this movement if you will, but then, isn't that what the British did for decades before the American Revolution?

Struggle and Private Student Loans

TO: JULIE M. WHITE, WELLS FARGO

Hi Julie,

I am glad to have an opportunity to share something about how Wells Fargo impacted my family. Shortly after my baby was born, she got very ill. Insurance did not cover most expenses. I put bills on my credit card. Things spiraled out of control. I had to declare bankruptcy to make a new start (which is going in a positive direction now, some years later).

But guess what: the private student loan I held with Wells Fargo was non-dischargeable. My co-signer is paying it off. Imagine what a difference it would have made to him and to my new start to have that included in the bankruptcy. Doesn't seem very fair, does it, to have one type of debt singled out like that.

I hope you will do what you can to speak up for women like me!

Thanks!

Jodi, mom to two great kids!

Wells Fargo Foreclosure

I am a hardworking mom of two teenagers. I was married for eighteen years before my marriage fell apart. My soon-to-be-ex lost his job of twenty-five years at UPS. I was not able to make the mortgage payments to Wells Fargo on my income alone.

I wrote to Wells Fargo Mortgage, asking for assistance—any help at all to keep me in my house and help me make the payments. I filled out all required paperwork, sometimes multiple times—all to no avail! No program was able to help me—not Wells Fargo's programs, not Obama's programs. Wells Fargo ended up foreclosing and changing the locks on my home in about nine months' time. My children and I are now renters for the first time in twenty-two years. I also went before the bankruptcy court today. And I make "good" money—a little more than $50,000 a year. If I can't make it and keep my home, how are those who make even less than me surviving?

Dear Sir, Your Company Sucks and Will Never See My $300

I know $300 is nothing to you, but despite joining the American workforce at age 15 (and receiving my diploma with the rest of my class, no need for applause), $300 is still a lot of money in my family. It could mean the difference of whether we eat during any two week period.

And this is despite the fact that my wife and I both have decent jobs, considering the town we live in.

What's my point? According to your company, I have owed Wells Fargo $300 for about seven years now. I opened my account in 1999 when I was 20 years old, and I was generally satisfied with our business relationship. But I continued to notice a decline in the quality at Wells Fargo over the years. You know, when all that overdraft fee racket started becoming a popular business model (don't pretend you don't know what I'm talking about).

And there would be irregularities and inconsistencies with the "digital" accounting of my debit card purchases that would result in unwarranted and possibly fraudulent overdraft fees. When that happened, I would point it out to a local branch manager, he would agree, and promptly fix that "misunderstanding." It wasn't until sometime in 2004 or 2005 that I came in and was informed that Wells Fargo had a new policy to no longer correct such errors. And then I had no choice but to pay those fees.

I am an honest person who has lived check to check for most of my life—some of my own fault, but also shaken down by such shady practices. So no, I will never bank with your company ever again. I used to love Wells Fargo and be proud to bank there.

Peace,

We are the 99%

Secretary of Labor

TO: ELAINE CHAO, WELLS FARGO

Ms. Chao,

You were Secretary of Labor in the Bush administration.* The Bush years were singularly bad years for
American workers. Stagnant wages drove families to
pull equity from their homes and run up credit card
debt, leaving them extremely vulnerable when the housing bubble burst and the deregulated financial system
collapsed.

Do you care about American labor? Workers, who
are out of jobs across this nation? How is serving on the
board helping Labor? Here's an idea—please advocate for
Labor representation on corporate boards! How about
following the German model and having an equal number of board seats reserved for workers? Now that is what
a Labor Secretary should support! Go Labor!

Sincerely,

Ann Burruss
Lafayette, Louisiana 70506

---

* From 2001 to 2009, Elaine Chao was Secretary of Labor in
the George W. Bush administration. Her husband is Republican
US Senator Mitch McConnell of Kentucky.

New Fees Since Wells Fargo Purchase of Wachovia

TO: JOHN G. STUMPF, WELLS FARGO

Dear Chairman John Stumpf,

Ever since Wells Fargo bought Wachovia I get an extra piece of mail each month. Like the prior sixteen years, I get the same Wachovia statement. But now I also receive a bill from Wells Fargo Bank. The bill is an add-on fee for the very modest line of credit that I have had at Wachovia, which never charged for this service. You don't want much: $25 per year. But it is the principle of the thing.

I used to earn a little interest on the funds I have in both a checking and a savings account, but now that has trickled down so much—given such low interest rates—I could barely buy a few postage stamps with that during the course of a year. Really, I am not sure I could buy more than two postage stamps. One of which I would have to use to send your bank the payment, which in my opinion is an overcharge.

Already Wachovia/Wells Fargo is making interest off of my money in my accounts. Given the fact that my taxpayer support bailed out your bank a few years ago, *and* the bank is already making high profits, and you get over $12 million in bonuses, I believe this fee is an unnecessary charge.

Frankly, Mr. Stumpf, the point of having money in a bank is that the customer collects a little interest. Use your old noggin. I pay Wells Fargo $25 a year, I go back-wards. Makes no sense.

So, I am not paying this added fee. Wells Fargo could save a little money on postage and not send me a new version of this bill each month.

New Fees

TO: JOHN G. STUMPF, WELLS FARGO

Dear Mr. Stumpf,

Once upon a time my father was able to walk into our local bank and be immediately recognized, greeted by name, offered a chair, and given prompt, competent service. This enduring relationship was the basis of our family's independent fortunes as they swelled and con-tracted over the decades.

I moved to California in 1995 and have been a loyal Wells Fargo customer ever since.

Recently, I received notice of the creation of new monthly fees attached to my checking account. I can tell you right now, in the current economy, I sadly cannot guarantee a minimum $1,500 balance, especially during the winter months, which are the slowest.

It is unclear how I might be damaging your com-pany's bottom line to deserve this monthly penalty. Your company appears to want to punish hardworking and still self-employed, self-supporting persons trying to survive in a depression. Is it Wells Fargo's unwritten policy to fleece customers at their most vulnerable hour?

I may have to say goodbye to Wells Fargo when this latest "fee" kicks in. The credit unions may be less "convenient," but they certainly let me keep my money. In these times, escaping your "fee" will actually make a difference when it comes time to eat. Something you perhaps cannot fathom.

If you have any leverage as an executive to help your long-term customers in the current climate, I certainly would appreciate that you waive these fees.

Thanks.

Congratulations, Mr. Stumpf!

TO: JOHN G. STUMPF, WELLS FARGO

Dear Mr. Stumpf,

I just wanted to write you a message, because I wanted to make sure you were aware of just how well your bank is doing in exceeding last year's numbers of $4.9 billion in bank account fees!

I work two jobs (retail and freelance) to keep up with my student loan payments ($700/month), mortgage ($1,100/month), utilities, insurance, credit, and two car payments ($1,500/month). I have so many payments, sometimes my account gets really low, and I like to pretend it's a game to see if my paycheck will clear in time before the payment goes through! It's very exciting, and when I lose, *you win*! Thirty dollars each time! And then, if I forget to check my account balance before doing something silly, like getting a cup of coffee so I don't fall asleep driving, or getting really hungry and having to eat something, *you* win even more! I don't ever do it on purpose, but that's okay. I still get breakfast, don't wreck from being tired, and I'm helping you to exceed last year's numbers!

Congratulations on all your success! May you do beautiful things with it!

Why I Am So Disappointed

TO: PATRICIA R. CALLAHAN, WELLS FARGO

A couple weeks ago, I was at a military grocery store (commissary) waiting to pay for my items. I was active duty military, and can tell you the honor it feels to serve America—the home of the greatest fighting forces on the planet.

In front of me at the cashier was a young military couple and their child. Long story short, the couple did not have enough money to pay for their food. In a country where we are to support our troops, our troops are worrying about supporting themselves.

Is this your fault? No. Why am I writing to you? For two reasons. One, they were using your debit card. And two, corporations like you have *nickel and dimed* everyone—and that is perhaps the greatest travesty of my generation.

New fees, ATM fees, overdraft fees—even your fees have fees. If for no one else, can you *at least* make it easier for America's fighting forces to feed their families? Shareholder profit—what about shareholder compassion and goodwill?

Fair Shares

It's OK to Be Rich

It isn't OK to pay less in taxes than your secretary does.

Wall St. 99 Percenters

I am one of the 99% poor, and even though I can't go to the Wall St. area because of my disability (I am 83 and can hardly walk or stand up), my heart is with them and I hope they will accomplish a lot.

It is ridiculous that the rich aren't taxed, and we all are. I wish ex-president Bush and his cronies were all put in jail for deleting taxes for the rich. More important, however, is pushing through President Obama's work bill. OWS, keep fighting!

Norma Goodman
Brooklyn, NY 11211

Fair Share

I have a friend who is a corporate lawyer and another who runs a hedge fund. Back in 2009, I heard them complaining about general criticism of the Wall Street bailouts, and I heard my hedge fund friend say that, despite the economic turmoil created by the subprime mortgage crisis, he was continuing to make big money on the backs of investors who, in turn, were somehow profiting from the downturn.

Then I heard my corporate lawyer friend talking about a millionaire's tax, saying, "But how much is too much? I am the one that generated that money . . . I worked harder than the average shmoe to get it. I paid for the colleges that got me the degrees I needed and got me my big job and my big house with a pool in the suburbs and allowed for my family's entry into exclusive schools and country clubs . . . why should I have to pay $300,000 a year in taxes? That's too much."

My argument then was the same as it is now: to the hedge fund guy, I say you are corrupt, criminal, and profiting off the misfortunes and misery of others—and someone should take you down. To the lawyer, I say you got what you got because of the security and stability of this country—you went to public schools as a kid, you benefited from roads and libraries and firehouses and police that were all paid for with public dollars—you did not achieve your success in a vacuum. Pay your fair share!

[Name withheld]
Manhattan, NY 10036

Pay for the Privilege of Doing Business in America

It seems that one of the extraordinary things about doing business and residing in the US is the ability to make money and benefit from the privileges of all things American. So the trouble my family and I have with corporations who will not pay significant taxes is that they are, in essence, welfare cheats. Using our system without supporting it is dishonorable and immoral.

Please, do the right thing and stop finding loopholes, and stop buying your way into American political decision-making to get more rules that benefit corporate profit. What is, in the end, the goal? Look at the destruction it is wreaking in schools, in our country's future and stability. Business can still turn a profit—perhaps a more stable profit—by doing the right thing and being a responsible part of society. What's more, it'll "buy" your good name and customer loyalty.

There's too much complexity to write here in a short note, but the main point is that you must take on a sense of personal connection and ethical responsibility to American society, to our country's functioning, and the first step to that is to stop getting out of paying your share of taxes, and stop influencing elections with massive contributions. We need to act like the people we want others to be, right?

G. Burton
Delaware, OH

To the 1%

All we are asking is that you pay your fair share of taxes. People are hurting and children are going hungry. If you have a heart, please help those of us who are not rich and are unemployed. Remember what God said, "the meek shall inherit the earth." Get right with God before it's too late.

Connie Moreno
Merrillville, IN 46410

Fairness

Dear Executives,

I work full-time; I do what many people consider to be a difficult job, working with mentally ill people, and I get $32,000 a year. You work a job and you get probably at least twenty times what I get. Is that fair? Is your job twenty times harder than mine?

You people seem to feel you are entitled to these ridiculous salaries. It's not fair for so many to be living in dire poverty while you are filthy rich.

Grow up! Get a conscience! We're all in this together!

Sincerely,

Mike Harburg
Olympia, WA 98506

Two Line Message

How hard or how long did you work to jeopardize the livelihoods of so many? Not nearly as long or hard as so many of us have and do everyday just to feed our families.

Krystle Knight
Houston, TX 77080

Extremism

You have benefited from government just as much as the welfare recipients, so I figure you owe America some payback.

James E. Shifflett Jr.
Charlottesville, VA 22903

Go Galt!

By god, you folks should just do it.

Go Galt!

These unruly ingrates of the Occupy movement just don't understand what a tough job you have.

Why, who would run the computers? The Markets? The Commodities Desk?

I say to you, with all of these rubes in such an uproarious mood, you should just do what the Masters of the Universe would do if the moochers and looters were making life difficult for innovators and job creators: Go Galt. Disappear. Just take your ball and go home. Let someone else try to make this all work.

Please. Take my advice.

I'm certain you're irreplaceable. You've said so yourselves.

So, just go.

And if you take this sage advice, know that this sentiment is from the heart:

You. Will. Not. Be. Missed.

Yours in truthiness,

Joey Sampson
Overland Park, KS 66212

$60,000 a year is not poor

TO: EDITH W. COOPER, GOLDMAN SACHS

Hi Edith,

Recently I was chatting with a former investment bank employee who is about to re-enter the job market after taking time off for a couple of years. She was discussing the job offers she's received, saying that she's not interested in getting back on the fast track after taking time off, and without thinking, tossed out a rough number for the compensation she expects for a job that is admittedly not the most challenging for someone with her background.

Edith, I was shocked. This compensation was more than three times what the highest earning member of my family makes—a family member with advanced degrees in engineering and business.

This person went on to dismiss the idea of another job, saying that she could do it but it would be the same amount of work and she would be "poor"—a salary that is almost three times the poverty level for a family of four. (I later heard an interview where a fellow revealed that this is what employees in the mailroom of his bank make.)

The idea that someone—intelligent and talented, but not a genius or an ambitious entrepreneur—could have this frame of reference for compensation is upsetting to me, and indicative of the larger problem we face. $60,000 a year is not poor—in fact, it's more than the median household income in New York state in 2009.

Adjusted for inflation, most Americans are making the same money now as they did in the late 1960s.

I would have been fine with bonuses and generous compensation packages for CEOs if they had been tied to the creation of actual value in the economy—value that was shared somehow with the people on whose backs it was created. Within the banks themselves, it seems like this is done—employees of the banks seem to be sharing in the profits of those banks. That's laudable.

But the banks seem to have forgotten that it wasn't solely the intelligence and hard work of their officers and employees that created (and held on to) much of the value created during the bubble. As has been catalogued elsewhere, the banks owe a huge debt to the US taxpayer for the money they were lent, the lenient scrutiny they received during the stress tests, and the lax regulatory environment that allowed them to get creative in the marketplace (sometimes with disastrous results).

We just want to share in the profits we helped to create. Not in some sort of one-time cash infusion, à la a CEOs bonus, but in lending practices that will stimulate business growth, a renewed commitment to ethical trading and rating practices, and a real commitment to making our country great again.

I Can Live Without a Stockbroker

I can live without a stockbroker, or a redundant financial advisor, but I can't live without a plumber, or the guy who picks up the trash, or who fixes the street, the electrician, the grocer, or the farmer (preferably local and organic). So, good riddance to you guys.

Sari Sarlund
Los Angeles, CA 90026

I Am

Omaha, Nebraska

TO: MICHAEL J. HEID, WELLS FARGO

Dear Mr. Banker,

I am a college graduate. I have taken a job as a waiter. I have been paying my student loans for about seven years. I owed about $28,000. I have been paying $344 a month for seven years. Which means I have paid $28,896. Give or take. You know what my balance is? $42,841.

This is what I think is messed up. I work as a waiter. There are no jobs for me. If things were different, education wouldn't do this to a person—put them in further debt. And with all these big companies taking jobs overseas and buying politicians to help themselves, what about me? When is enough enough? Banks shouldn't make such huge profits off education.

Rich to Richard Parsons

TO: RICHARD D. PARSONS, CITIGROUP

Hi Richard!

I live in Bed-Stuy, where you got your start. I have waited on you many times and served you wine. I always found you pleasant, and thought this could be a rare way to ask for your help in supporting revolutionary change in this country.

I am writing to ask your support for Occupy Wall Street. It would be wonderful to have your help in furthering our goals as they form. The Buffett Rule, ending predatory lending, tightening regulations on derivatives trading, eliminating the power of lobbyists, taking corporate interests out of politics, ending the FED, and a whole host of other goals are in the works. *Please* be on the right side of things and help *reform* your corporate culture of greed and deception!

Richard, can you please help us and call off the lobbyists in Washington and let us have our democracy back?

Here is the kind of system we dream of having . . . it would be a much more humane way of creating policy than using money to influence lawmakers! http://www.youtube.com/watch?v=6dtD8RnGaRQ!

Enjoy your dinners of nice food and wine in Tribeca! Lots of us work hard to make you comfortable. Maybe you can return the favor and help *reform* the unethical practices and predatory lending that brought our nation to its knees?

Hope to see you soon!

Thanks!!

Rich
Brooklyn, NY

I Am the 99%

I work, I pay taxes, and I'm mad as hell. I am not a socialist, I am not an anarchist, and I am not an aging hippie. I am a 42-year-old mother, wife, daughter, sister, aunt, and friend who is sick and tired of seeing people struggling so damn hard to get by in this country and around the world. When will "you people" realize that everything is connected? That we are all one? Every choice you make has a consequence—and it's holding hands with your profit.

Live Free or Die!

[Name withheld]
New Hampshire

Contrary to What You People Think

Contrary to what you people think, we are not a bunch of free-sex druggies who have nothing but time on our hands. We are the reality of middle and lower-class folks, working and retired, teachers, lawyers, entrepreneurs, under- and unemployed, writers, farmers . . . you name us! We are sick and tired of the control you exert on our lives and livelihoods!

I'm a 57-year-old builder/craftsman who has raised four children, one of whom served this country in Iraq, came home with PTSD, married, has a child, goes to school, works part-time, cares for his child, and struggles daily with his anxiety and depression. Two other children work and go to university with little help from parents who can't afford to help. My oldest son works for a utility company and has three children. The lot of us struggle with bills, budgets, etc., and know we've been dispossessed.

We are all committed to fighting greed and avarice. Avarice is a disease that you've succumbed to. You're infected with this undesirable quality and are useless to mankind. Your exploits are being exposed and those you've enslaved are uniting to plunder your domain.

99 Percenter Speaking

To all my Wall Street and other boardroom "friends": I trust that I can address you as friends, since we are all human beings on this planet.

I am an 80-plus-year-old fortunate widow, since I actually do own modest amounts of stock in a few large companies. For many years, I have voted proxies, trying to make a statement in favor of smaller salaries and bonuses for top executives, along with other progressive causes. Obviously, this has been to no avail. I am so encouraged by the present outpouring of similar sentiments all over our nation and around the world. I trust you are all listening and heeding the hopes of us all. Most sincerely and respectfully,

Rosa Julstrom
Chicago, IL 60640

Have We Abandoned All Sense of Decency and Ethical Judgment, Sir?

I am a recent UC Berkeley graduate who accumulated $18,000 of debt while financing my entire educational expenses. My family was unable to support me financially because we fell into the same cracks that many other families of the working poor fall into: my parents earned just enough to disqualify them from public aid, but not enough to afford the privilege of a health insurance plan or an adequate education for their children.

In spite of the structural and cultural disadvantages that come with being part of a historically marginalized community, my parents worked their hardest to keep our heads above water. Now you tell me, is it fair that *nobody* attempted to bail out families like mine while bankers like yourself took almost $1 trillion of taxpayer money and then rewarded yourselves with exorbitant bonuses? Is it fair that the same people who created the 2008 financial crisis were rewarded instead of punished?

We must face the fact that we live in a highly stratified society where social class determines where you live, where you work, and where your kids go to school, which in turn can either improve or hurt one's life chances. All ideologies and politics aside, we are at a crucial crossroads where we can help reduce the effects of social and economic injustice by extending health care and other public amenities to address racial and social inequality, or we can continue to support a system that privileges status and wealth while depriving marginalized communities from the basic means to compete for such status and wealth.

As a member of a subordinate group who has experienced segregation, I wish to ask what your colleagues and associates in the White House think of the fact that we still have ethnic ghettos or "inner cities" that will be perpetually disenfranchised if we continue to defund crucial public services that provide vital support for these communities.

I will leave you with this passage from Martin Luther King:

Whenever this issue of compensatory or
preferential treatment for the Negro
is raised, some of our friends recoil
in horror. The Negro should be granted
equality they agree; but he should ask for
nothing more. On the surface, this appears
reasonable, but it is not realistic. For it
is obvious that if a man is entered at the
starting line in a race three hundred years
after another man, the first would have to
perform some impossible feat in order to
catch up with his fellow runner.

—Dr. Martin Luther King Jr., <u>Why We Can't Wait</u>

A Stint at McDonald's Would Be Good for Your Soul

I am a 69-year-old grandmother. My husband has Alzheimer's and will soon need care that is not covered by Medicare. My daughter and grandson have TBI (traumatic brain injuries) from a terrible car accident. She has to work in constant pain and with little short-term memory. He has not been able to return to school or work. My cousin has Parkinson's and has been out of work for four years. Another cousin's daughter died because she did not have insurance and went to the hospital too late to be stabilized. My nephew just came back from Afghanistan with a purple heart; he was filled with shrapnel and we counted him lucky. This was his fifth deployment. I don't think he met your children there.

We, the 99%, have all become impoverished while you, the 1%, have so much. It's hard to see how you can go to sleep at night. I would sleep better if banks were heavily regulated and you were incarcerated and made to forgo your ridiculous income. Fieldwork or a stint at McDonald's would be good for your soul.

Linda Laird
KS Granny

I Have No Sob Story Myself

Hello there,

I have no sob story myself. I live a good life within my means, and I am lucky. However, I worry about the future of our country with such a huge income gap between the few and the many. If you, the very wealthy, are indeed able to preserve this way of living, you may have ten beautiful homes, cheap labor to work for you, and inexpensive gas to fuel the giant vehicle that will drive you through all the smelly, polluted, and crumbling societies living closer and closer to your front door. You will eventually be a very rich man living in a very poor country. That would suck, don't you agree?

Thank you for considering these thoughts.

I Am a Blind 74-Year-Old Retired Social Worker

I am a blind 74-year-old retired social worker. For thirty-four years, I had a private practice and worked as an independent contractor with adoption agencies. I owned my own home and invested my money in municipal bonds. I assumed that when I had to retire, my social security, investment income, and Medicare benefits would keep me financially secure until my death. I did not expect to live in luxury or own a retirement home; I just expected to not have to worry about paying for my living expenses and medical care.

Now, because of the financial crises brought on by the deregulation of banking and investment and the greed of bankers, financial institutions, and transnational corporations, I live with constant anxiety about my future. My living costs are rising. I take many necessary medications and the costs for their co-pays are rising incredibly. Social security benefits are being threatened even though this is a self-sustaining program. Medicare benefits may be cut. Premiums for supplemental Medicare insurance are rising.

My financial future was profoundly affected because the housing bubble was bursting just as I had to put my house on the market. And my story is hardly the saddest you will hear if you choose to listen. You live in another world and are personally affected by none of this. But it is only a matter of chance that you are there and 99% of us are here. Please think about our common humanity rather than profit and power.

Miriam Vieni
Westbury, NY 11590

Jail Time for Both Wall Street and Bank Criminals

I am a longtime conservative who voted for Ronald Reagan twice over.

I have had it with you bastards. My daughter and her husband lost a full one-third of their 401(k) in your stock market while those who squandered their savings walked away with bonuses numbering in the millions.

As a 73-year-old retired professional, I am proud of those young people who are now marching on Wall Street.

You bastards have it coming and I hope and pray that you all wind up in jail.

I will also make this known to both our member of Congress and Senate and will vote based on whether they take immediate action against you gangsters.

Thomas Mathews
Auburn, PA 17922

The Impact of Recklessness

I am appalled at the hubris. I carry mail and have never in twenty years seen the number of unemployed so high. These are not ne'er-do-wells or slackers. These are ordinary, hardworking, middle-class workers who have faithfully put in each day at their respective jobs. It is no fault of theirs that the decisions of greedy bankers, hedge funds, and their shareholders pulled the economy out from under their feet. Those who acted in this manner knew better. Our incomes, pensions, and hopes should not have been recklessly disregarded. Those of us in the real world would have been seriously punished for neglect of duty.

Your actions have affected the postal service too. Our commercial accounts have been severely impacted. The standard mail supports the reasonable prices and ongoing stability of our business. It is affecting all sectors.

We in the real world don't get bailed out. We have to figure a way out. Our options are few and dwindling.

Think of someone other than yourself!

Cheryl R. Barlow
Rockford, IL 61104

Student Loan

I'm writing you as I am waiting to be heard in a court-room in Queens, New York. I'm here fighting an eviction. I get $200 a month taken out of my paycheck because I am in default in my loans. I take home $1,500 after taxes and my rent is $1,200, which is considered cheap in NYC. Those $200 would allow me to pay my rent. Thanks.

Fernando
Kew Gardens, NY 11415

I Have a Full-Time Job with Benefits

I have a full-time job with benefits. So does my husband. We both graduated from a top university and are recognized by both our seniors and our peers as leaders in our fields, and our careers reflect that. Yet, when my gynecologist found a growth in my pelvis, and even though I have a strong family history of cancer, I could not afford to get it checked out—despite having health insurance. My $4,000 (yes, *thousand*) deductible and 20% co-pay for all procedures after $4,000, and the absolute inability to determine beforehand what procedures and tests I'd be given and how much each would cost (despite repeated calls to my insurance company), meant that all of our savings could be wiped out by following my gynecologist's prescription to receive further testing. After one surprise bill following a workplace injury last year, I am too afraid to take that chance.

I have done everything right—*am* doing everything right. My husband and I both have good jobs that pay us more than many of our friends earn. Yet I still cannot afford basic health care—diagnosis of a possibly fatal disease.

Even if you do not run a health care-related company, I have a feeling you can probably guess why prices are increasing while access to care is decreasing. I bet at your institution as well, there are higher prices for a lower quality and quantity of service. And I bet that's great news to you—as long as your shareholders and board members are happy, right?

America once was a country of companies that wanted to be the best at producing or providing whatever good or service they specialized in. Now those companies just want to be the richest. That means it's a country where we, the ones who must use those products, are no longer valued. It is no longer a country where we can live; it is only a country where we can hope to survive.

Laura Easley
North Bergen, NJ 07047

I Have Worked Hard All My Life

Dear 1%,

I have worked hard all my life. I grew up in foster care because my father had a drinking problem and my mother was completely dependent on him. These are the ways people cope with the struggles in the system you work in. You only care about profits, not people. Thank God I was able to know that my father beating me and drinking was not okay. I ran away from home. I was homeless until I was able to find a home in foster care. I have a good head on my shoulders.

I was unable to attend college. After turning 18, I went to work and worked two jobs. I gave my free time to working as a volunteer firefighter. I wanted so badly to be a firefighter in New York City or in my hometown of Rochester. That dream did not come true. Instead, I got a job at Delphi making auto parts. I work hard, very hard. I made $14/hour. I am a UAW member.

Again, your policies attack my family. You attack unions and try to break them just so you can make more profits. My union is all I have of a family. It's given me everything you don't want me to have: dignity, a voice in my workplace, a roof over my head, and friends to talk to when I feel alone in the absence of family.

I know I am wasting my time trying to ask you to stop pulling apart my family. I know that, at the end of the day, you sleep well with a bought family. Money buys everything, right? Is that why you do what you do to America and the rest of the world? If you have more money, you can buy more friends and family.

I have 99%. You have 1%. I feel sad for you. My friends and family are true and plenty. We will fight to protect our families and our friends until ethics return to our country and to our world. You will not break us. We are awake to what is going on and until it ends, we will occupy everything.

Lynn Giglio
Pavilion, NY 14525

Measuring Up

To the 1%,

I am a retiree who spent many years teaching students not only subject matter but self-respect, respect for others, and measuring up. My students were inner-city and immigrants. They loved learning and being told that they could do it, and they did.

Now, you tell me that I should just curl up and die—without Medicare, Social Security, or even a pension. I went to school for many years, got a Master's degree and far more than thirty credits beyond so that I could keep my job. I started to work at age 16.

I did not worship the Golden Calf. Otherwise, I would never have become a teacher. My ability to respect myself and my contribution to the world are priceless. I deserve to keep what I worked long and hard for.

Do you deserve your huge compensation? Can you look me in the eye and say that you respect yourself and your contribution? Are you only leaving behind a destroyed environment and spiritual bankruptcy?

Leathea Vanadore
New York, NY 10001

You Should Take a Pay Cut and Donate Part of Your Salary

My name is Stephanie and I am a single mom with a teen and a baby and we live in NYC in a shelter. It's been two years that I have been homeless. I am homeless not because I didn't pay my bills, not because of drugs. . . . I am homeless because both my parents died and I was living in their co-op and was kicked out by the church.

I am angry that there are no jobs. I am angry that there are no housing programs. I am angry that I have no help. I am angry that the rich keep getting richer and the poor keep getting poorer. Look around and see all the homeless people. The hungry people. Look and see how many homeless kids there are. Something *must* be done!

Stephanie Brandt
New York, NY 10025

Old, Tired, and My Back Hurts

I am old, tired, and my back hurts *but* I am joining OWS.

Coda

The Declaration of Independence Had Twenty-Seven Grievances

Don't criticize the protesters for not having a single cause. The founding fathers had twenty-seven, and look what happened.

The Game of Monopoly

We used to play Monopoly a lot as kids. Eventually one player would amass almost all the houses, hotels, and cash in the game—and the game would come to a halt. At that point we had two options. Either we could quit and go do something else, or the holder of all the loot could redistribute the wealth so we could all continue to play.

You and yours have evidently not learned that lesson. You play, not with tokens and toy money, but with the resources of the earth and the lives of people. You are coming very close to hoarding all the property and money, and just as in Monopoly, the game is grinding to a halt. The problem, of course, is that in this particular version of the game, there is no quitting because there is nowhere else to go and nothing else to do. Good planets are rather scarce.

My brother used to insist on being banker in our Monopoly games. I finally figured out why he always won. Money paid out by the bank came out of the bank. Money paid into the bank somehow ended up in his personal stash—a lot like what you have been doing these past decades.

That puts us, the 99%, in a difficult position. Since quitting means lying down and dying, our only option is to wrest from you, the "winners," some portion of what you have taken from the rest of us. In economic parlance, you have internalized the benefits and externalized the costs. Those of us who pay the costs on a daily basis are reaching the end of both our ability to pay (again, the game is winding down) and our patience. We really don't think your continued affluence is worth dying for.

Trouble is, you have now expanded your empires to the point that those externalized costs are causing the breakdown of the entire planet. There are upwards of 3 million species whose survival depends on the continuation of a functional planetary ecosystem (think climate change). There are now 7 billion humans who also depend on that functional planetary ecosystem.

Even you, having hoarded almost all the natural and economic wealth in the world, need a functional planetary ecosystem to continue to live. Like the rest of us, you need air to breathe, clean water to drink, and productive land on which to grow the food you need.

It's time for some serious reassessment and reevaluation of your goals, purposes, and values.

Marianne Edain
Langley, WA 98260

Small Businesses Are the Economy

I'm a small business owner in New York City. We started in 2007, with nothing but determination and the ability to work hard. We've grown each year, despite a global recession and lack of access to credit. We pay our bills and taxes, and put the money we make back into our local economy. We have *more demand* than we can keep up with. My partner and I work 24/7 because we don't have cash on hand to hire the local employees we need to expand our business.

Why?

Because your banks—which took billions of dollars of our tax money in bailouts, and are able to borrow money at rock-bottom rates from our government in the name of "economic stimulus"—have *failed* to lend back to small businesses.

Because all our profits go to pay interest and bank and credit card fees. You get a percentage of every dollar our clients pay us. We operate month-to-month on a cash basis. We don't take excessive risks because we are responsible and don't depend on bailouts from our fellow citizens. We are working hard to build our own American Dream, playing by the rules.

Can any of your big banks and investment firms honestly say the same? What value do you create for anyone but your shareholders?

A small line of credit at a reasonable interest rate is all we need to hire people and *create jobs*. I'm sick of hearing about "job creators" who are punishing our entire country for your own risky behavior.

A healthy economy needs consumers with money to spend. Sucking all the money up into your offshore accounts is insanely short-sighted. Even if you and your kids live comfortably behind walled gates, you cannot be separate from the world. Wake up!

C. Mahoney
New York City, 10031

Please Enjoy Yourselves; You Deserve It

I've been reflecting on my past forty-one years working as a contractor since I was discharged from the USAF in 1969, as I am now waiting for the bank to come and take my home from me. I've concluded that it was your doing, you along with the best government your money could buy, that did this to me, and I wonder what you will do with this prime piece of real estate. You already live in the best residences money can buy, and vacation in places where you never have to give me a thought, so you will probably sell it to another up-and-coming 1 percenter and he'll take advantage of all the upgrades and renovations on the property—which I watched over for six years before it came on the market and then lovingly fixed up, so it would serve me in my declining years and perhaps be my son's to use as he starts his life someday. . . Well, it was just a thought. So enjoy yourselves and maybe I'll send you a housewarming gift to welcome you to my neighborhood.

Michael Iverson
Snohomish, WA 98296

Casino Politics

It's very easy to steal from the poor: they have no political clout and have little recourse via expensive legal teams. So it's no wonder that creating risky loans for the housing industry, directly marketed to the poor, which were expected to be defaulted on, would result in the current economic mess. Especially when all the financial institutions *knew* well beforehand that the government would bail them out.

You people created this mess, and America hates you for it. You socialized the losses and privatized the gains in your disgusting Casino Economics. I spit upon your virtual feet.

The 1 %

I'm depressed and horrified by the disintegration of values that Wall Street, the banks, and the CEOs have demonstrated.

And I truly don't understand how you have ignored the potential of a healthy middle class that has been proven vital to a nation's overall health. I've been an executive and I know that many people don't understand the responsibility and challenges that kind of position brings. However, what has happened over the last two years has far exceeded any recompense due those positions.

You have not only disenfranchised the middle class, you have also created a surge of anger that is picking up speed and can only result in massive conflict and outbreaks of violence in the end. I suppose that you feel protected by the dollars you've accumulated, but ultimately, even that won't help. You are destroying America's future, not just for the 99%, but for your own children with your greed and indifference.

We have entered into a new age, taking a quantum leap in how people think, and I personally have seen schools around the country where students have little or no equipment at all to move forward, to develop their potential and the possibilities for this nation to thrive.

Considering current conditions, who do you think will be able to buy the products made by the corporations you fund? How will those goods be transported when infrastructure is crumbling? Who will be capable, due to education and basic needs met, of creating the solutions that we will need to go forward? Who will buy American products when they can buy products from other countries? Who will deposit money in banks, except for yourselves and foreign investors, and who once the latter's investments exceed yours? In the end, who will serve you in your homes when you're sick and malnourished and resentful? Perhaps you're operating in part out of your own fear, because you do see the writing on the wall.

The greatest challenges we face today are resistance to change, the poison of what we eat and drink and breathe, and the lack of support for collective creativity—the kind of creativity that is behind the very things that you buy and wish to have in your homes and business. Products that your families use.

It's obvious that what once may have worked is no longer valid. The system is crumbling and the harder we attempt to return to what once worked, the faster we'll fall.

You're short-sighted, and by no means visionaries. The price to be paid for all this will not leave you untouched.

I hope that at some point you will begin to understand and act on the fact that we are connected and that we need each other to survive and prosper. Currently, I see little, if anything, to indicate that your eyes have opened.

I find myself unable to end this with a time-honored "with respect," but sign it instead with,

Sincerely,

Sharon Crespi
Arlington, WA 98223

No Bailout Here

No one has paid my way. I have done it all by myself. Now I have $60,000 in student loans so I can teach low-income children how to read.

Did I get bailed out or have my home loan modified? Nope. I had to file for bankruptcy and am probably going to lose my home. I worked full-time as a secretary during the day and went to school at night to try and have the American Dream. Now I feel like that dream has been shattered, due to no one really caring about my needs for a home.

Yet I continue to believe that in America, all of this can't be happening. People somewhere must care!

No trust funds headed my way. No help here. Just more after-school tutoring in order to try and spare my home from foreclosure. The ten furlough days I had to take have not helped. But still I work hard for the kids in my class who deserve a teacher like me who loves and cares for them!

Karimeh Tuttle
Apple Valley, CA 92307

Time for Change

Wall Street needs to bail out Main Street, not the other way around.

Bernadine Turner
Newberry, FL 32669

So Tired and Scared for the Future

I am a 34-year-old woman with a graduate degree. I work full-time as a hospice social worker counseling dying people and their families. My husband is a 35-year-old small business owner as well as a student. We have two beautiful children.

We don't ask for much in life. We own a small home (that is now worth about half of what we purchased it for). We both drive old cars. We buy whatever we can at secondhand and thrift stores. We don't go out. We don't eat out. We contribute meager sums to a 403(b), hoping that the market doesn't wipe it out completely. We have virtually no other savings. We also have over $50,000 in credit card debt. We work *so hard* day in and day out, and we can never seem to get ahead.

We are not CEOs or "important people," but we value what we do and we believe it contributes value to society. We just want to live comfortably and without fear that our modest lifestyle and hopes for the future will be shattered. We just want a level playing field and the promise of the American Dream that we grew up believing in. We don't feel that we get a say in what happens in this country. That needs to change. That is the message that OWS is trying to send to you. *We are the 99%.*

Dear 1%

Every day, my husband and I work very hard for the money we make so that we can survive. After we pay our bills, we may have enough to eat out or take the kids to the movies. Our family of four lives in a 100-year-old, 1,200-square foot house with one bathroom. My husband loads planes all day; I teach a toddler classroom. Then at night, I do online school and my husband goes to work at UPS so that we can have health insurance. I don't think you could live my life for more than one week. What would I do if I was you? Start downsizing my own life and give money to charities and people who really need it!

Marnie Cedillos
Denver, CO 80220

If You Only Knew. . .

If you only knew what the rest of us felt, how the rest of us felt. If only you had to witness your parents shutter their proud, family-owned business of thirty-two years because they could no longer finance the operation. If only you had to watch as your 62-year-old parents were forced to look and interview for new jobs after owning their own business for over three decades. If only your mother had to choose between paying the family's bills and purchasing her thyroid medication. If only your son had to go years without eyeglasses because he couldn't afford them . . . even after graduating from a Big Ten university and a law school, only to be on unemployment and crushed by $180,000 in student loan debt. If only your sister had to plead with a bank teller to reverse a $30 overdraft fee based on a 28 cent overdraft . . . in public and in front of a dozen customers and staff. If only you could not go out with friends on a Friday night because you did not have the money to even pay the $5 cover charge. If only you ran out of gas on the highway three miles from your house in negative ten degree weather simply because you didn't get paid until tomorrow. If only you knew. If only you understood.

Adam Spees
Minneapolis, MN 55413

Compassion and Patriotism

Patriotism is everyone doing what they can to revive the country. Why don't you have any? Compassion for those less fortunate is just human. Why don't you have any? Using our savings as your safety net has pissed America off. If people can bring down corrupt governments they can certainly bring down corrupt institutions. A new way of doing business is in your future.

Wallace Rhodes
Los Angeles, CA

Money

We bail you out with our hard earned money, you still treat us like crap.

Lester Begay
Farmington, NM 87499

Lucky Me!

From a blue-collar background in the Bronx, I landed a Teamster job at an air freight company in Los Angeles. I met my significant other there and in 1979, we bought a house in a very affluent beach community for $95,000. For thirty-two years I had complete health coverage for which I paid nothing—no monthly, no co-pay. At that time, I retired at the age of 54 with full pension and benefits for which I now pay a nominal amount. The "powers that be" would have you believe that people like me [unionized workers] and my public sector brothers and sisters are the reason for the financial mess we're in to deflect attention from their own complicity. I am the 99%. I am what the middle class is all about.

Laura Cipollari
Manhattan Beach, CA 90266

We Are Three Professionals

We are three professionals who ran a very profitable business in Las Vegas. Due to your crass corruption, we were financially forced to move back to our Indian Reservation. We no longer contribute a goodly amount to the US tax system. Banksters are enemies of democracy.

Delaine Spilsbury
McGill, NV 89318

401(k)

Bailing out your businesses has devalued my savings and sentenced me to another decade of work.

Lawrence Brown
Franksville, WI 53126

Consumer and Investor Perspective

Just because I have used your products or hold shares in your companies doesn't mean I give you permission to do *anything* to advance the profit line for your company. I do not give you my permission to lobby Congress or help fund election campaigns. I do not give you my permission to take actions or promote products that destroy the environment and our health, create mass unemployment, and line the pockets of your CEOs with more than thirty times the income of your lowest paid employee. I do not give you permission to find and follow every avenue to avoid paying taxes. I do not give you permission to send your jobs abroad. I do not give you permission to invent financial schemes to create market manipulations that leave people's retirements on the floor and your profit skyrocketing, and I do not give you permission to align your interests with ALEC. I do not give you permission to offer mortgages based on false premises. I do not give you permission to foreclose on people who have paid their mortgages and who are trying to work out financial deals to stay in their homes. I do not give you permission to create an oligarchy or crony capitalism based on what's good for your CEOs and your bottom line and what's bad for the rest of us. I do not give you permission to follow policies that do not include social responsibility as your first priority and profit after that.

[Name withheld]
Alaska

A Planned Retirement at 65

My husband is 61 and I am 57. He was a business owner until 2001. In 2001 he changed careers. We had saved all our money in order to do this, and we had enough to work until a planned retirement at 65.

Our money was invested in the stock market, much of it in mutual funds. Our portfolio is worth less than half of what it would have been worth had the "money changers" on Wall Street not used the market like a huge casino. We can look forward to many more years of work, thanks to you. We are completely unable to retire.

My parents worked until ages 55 and 51 respectively. My father was a railroad yardmaster and my mother was a retail manager. They put two of us through college and still were able to retire young. They enjoyed more than thirty years of comfortable retirement.

My husband and I will likely never fully retire. He is in a job that is physically very demanding. I don't know how he is going to keep going.

Marilyn Scattoreggio
Dix Hills, NY 11746

An Invitation to Dinner at Our House

I, an unemployed mother of three, would like to invite you to have dinner at our house. But my invitation probably won't last too long because I will probably have my electricity turned off soon. My 4-week-old grandbaby, who is on oxygen, might have to be rushed to the hospital, but that is OK, because we will survive.

One good thing about unemployment and having all my children (who have also lost their jobs) and my two grandbabies living with me is that we qualify for food stamps. Seriously, I love to cook and as long as the food lasts, please join us for a Sunday dinner.

Thanks, and have a great day. . . I will . . . you can take our money, but you can't take our spirit.

Pen Pals

If this book of letters inspires you to write your own letters to executives and directors at American banks, we encourage you to do so. Headquarters and office addresses for official mail are listed below.

Occupy the Boardroom's original call for letters included a request that we would like to echo here: "We hope you become pals with [name here]—but be sure to do it in a constructive manner that helps build the movement for a better world. Do not intimidate, harass, or threaten anyone, no matter what you might think of them. Think funny! The #OWS movement emphasizes peaceful, non-violent protesting." In the box where people wrote their messages, OTBR added the further reminder: "Remember, be polite!"

The founders of the United States took hold of their anger and wrote the Declaration of Independence. They convinced and inspired. Maybe you will establish a correspondence with someone below. We believe the right word, offered at the right time, can change a life.

Bank of America Corporation

100 North Tryon Street
Charlotte, North Carolina 28255
United States of America

The following people hold management positions at Bank of America and can be reached at Bank of America's corporate address, above.

Bryan Moynihan
Chief Executive Officer, President, Director and Member of Executive Committee

Joe L. Price
Former President of Consumer and Small Business Banking

Barbara J. Desoer
President of Home Loans and Insurance

Charles H. Noski
Former Vice Chairman and Executive Vice President
Other affiliations: Morgan Stanley; Merrill Lynch & Co.; Microsoft Corporation

Gary G. Lynch
Global Chief of Legal, Compliance, and Regulatory Actions

Bruce R. Thompson
Chief Financial Officer

Edward P. O'Keefe
General Counsel

Thomas K. Montag
Co-Chief Operating Officer
Other affiliations: The Goldman Sachs Groups

David C. Darnell
Co-Chief Operating Officer

Neil Cotty
Chief Accounting Officer

Ron D. Sturzenegger
Legacy Asset Servicing Executive

Paula Ann Dominick
Interim Chief Risk Officer

Charles K. Gifford
Director, Chairman of Credit Committee and
Member of Executive Committee

Robert W. Scully
Independent Director, Chairman of Compensation &
Benefits Committee, and Member of Audit Committee

Charles O. Holliday, Jr.
Chairman of Executive Committee

Susan Schmidt Bies
Independent Director
*Other affiliations: Former Member of the Board of
Governors at the Federal Reserve*

D. Paul Jones, Jr.
Former Independent Director, Member of Audit
Committee, and Member of Corporate Governance
Committee

Anne M. Finucane
Global Strategy and Marketing Officer

Lawrence Di Rita
Spokesman
Other affiliations: acting Assistant Secretary of Defense for Public Affairs and US Department of Defense spokesman under Donald Rumsfeld

Andrea B. Smith
Global Head of Human Resources

Catherine P. Bessant
Global Technology and Operations Executive

Terrence P. Laughlin
Chief Risk Officer

Christine P. Katziff
Corporate General Auditor

The following are affiliated with Bank of America and can be reached at the addresses below:

Frank P. Bramble, Sr.
Director, Chairman of Enterprise Risk Committee, and Member of Corporate Governance Committee
College of Business and Economics
Towson University
8000 York Road
Towson, MD 21252

Thomas J. May
Director

Northeast Utilities
56 Prospect Street
Hartford, CT 06103

Monica C. Lozano
Director
Other affiliations: Member of President Obama's
Economic Recovery Advisory Board

Chief Executive Officer, ImpreMedia, LLC
700 South Flower Street
Suite 3000
Los Angeles, CA 90017

Charles O. Rossotti
Director
The Carlyle Group LP
1001 Pennsylvania Avenue, NW
Washington, DC 20004

Virgis W. Colbert
Director
Lorillard, Inc.
714 Green Valley Road
Greensboro, NC 27408

Mukesh Ambani
Director
Makers Chambers - IV
Nariman Point
Mumbai 400 021
India

Citigroup

399 Park Avenue
New York, New York 10043
United States of America

The following people hold management
positions at Citigroup and can be
reached at Citigroup's corporate
address, above.

Vikram S. Pandit
Chief Executive Officer and Director

William R. Rhodes
Senior Adviser

Manuela Medina-Mora
Chairman Global Consumer Banking and Chief
Executive Officer of Global Consumer Banking for the
Americas

Peter Orszag
Vice Chairman of Corporate and Investment Banking
*Other affiliations: Former Director of the Office of
Management and Budget under President Obama*

James Wolfensohn
Senior Advisor
*Other affiliations: Former Director of the Office of
Management and Budget under President Obama*

Michael Corbat
Chief Executive Officer, Europe, Middle East, and
Africa

Don Callahan
Chief Operations & Technology Officer and Chief
Administrative Officer

James A. Forese
Co-Chief Executive Officer of Investment Banking Unit

John P. Havens
President, Chief Operating Officer, and Chief Executive
Office of Institutional Clients Group

Brian Leach
Chief Risk Officer
Other affiliations: Morgan Stanley

John C. Gerspach
Chief Financial Officer

The following are affiliated with Citigroup and
can be reached at the addresses below:

Richard D. Parsons
Former Chairman of Citigroup

Senior Advisor, Providence Equity Partners, LLC
One Time Warner Center
New York, NY 10019

Nicholas Calio
Former Executive Vice President of Global Government Affairs

CEO of Airlines for America
1301 Pennsylvania Avenue,
NW, Suite 1100
Washington, DC 20004

Michael S. Helfer
Citigroup General Counsel and Corporate Secretary
201 Queens Avenue
London, Ontario N6A 1J1, Canada

Judith Rodin
Director

President, The Rockefeller Foundation
420 Fifth Avenue
New York, New York 10018

Alain J. P. Belda
Director

Managing Director and Member of Executive
Management Group, Warburg Pincus LLC
390 Park Avenue
New York, NY 10022

Robert L. Ryan
Director

Independent Director, Member of Finance Committee
and Member of Audit Committee, General Mills, Inc.
3000 Hanover Street
Palo Alto, CA 94304

Goldman Sachs

200 West Street
New York, New York 10282
United States of America

The following people hold management positions
at Goldman Sachs and can be reached at Goldman
Sachs' corporate address, above.

Lloyd C. Blankfein
Chairman, President and CEO

Gregory K. Palm
Goldman Sachs General Counsel

David A. Viniar
CFO, Executive Vice President

John S. Weinberg
Vice Chairman

Esta E. Stecher
General Counsel, Executive Vice President

Faryar Shirzad
Global Head of Government Affairs
*Other affiliations: Former Special and Deputy Assistant
to the President on the National Security Council*

Abby Joseph Cohen
Senior US Investment Strategist

David Heller
Co-Head of Securities Division
Announced retirement January 12, 2012

J. Michael Evans
Vice Chairman

Sarah G. Smith
Principal Accounting Officer

Michael S. Sherwood
Vice Chairman
Other affiliations: Co-Chief Executive Officer and Director of Goldman Sachs International

Alan M. Cohen
Executive Vice President

Edith W. Cooper
Executive Vice President

William W. George
Director

John H. Bryan
Director
Retired 2012

Gary D. Cohn
President, Chief Operating Officer, and Director

James A. Johnson
Director
Other affiliations: Fannie Mae

Stephen Friedman
Director
Other affiliations: Federal Reserve Bank of New York

Lois D. Juliber
Director
Other affiliations: MasterCard Foundation

Claes Dahlbäck
Director

James J. Schiro
Director

Lakshmi Mittal
Director

Debora Spar
Director

John F. W. Rogers
Executive Vice President, Chief of Staff, and Secretary
to the Board

JP Morgan Chase

270 Park Avenue
New York, NY 10017
United States of America

The following people hold management positions
at JP Morgan Chase & Co. and can be reached
at JP Morgan Chase & Co.'s corporate address,
above.

Jamie Dimon
Chief Executive Officer
Other affiliations: The Federal Reserve Bank of
New York

Jay Mandelbaum
Former Executive Vice President
Stepped down January 2012

Heidi Miller
Former Executive Vice President
Stepped down January 2012

Stephen M. Cutler
JP Morgan Chase General Counsel

James Staley
Head of Asset Management, Head of Investment
Banking, and Managing Director

Charles W. Scharf
Managing Director and Partner
Other affiliations: Visa USA, Inc.

Michael J. Cavanagh
Chief Executive Officer of Treasury and Securities
Services Business
Other affiliations: Bear Stearns Companies, LLC

Ina R. Drew
Former Chief Investment Officer
Stepped down in May 2012

Glenn F. Tilton
Executive and Chairman of Midwest Operations

Mel R. Martinez
Chairman of the Southeast and Latin America

Peter Scher
President of Corporate Responsibility

Blythe Masters
Head of Global Commodities

Jacob A. Frenkel
Chairman, JP Morgan International

Douglas Braunstein
Chief Financial Officer, Chairman of Investment
Committee, and Member of Operating Committee

Klaus Diederichs
Head of Investment Banking and Origination in
Europe, Middle East, and Africa

Barry Zubrow
Head of Corporate Regulatory Affairs

John L. Donnelly
Head of Human Resources

Frank Bisignano
Head of US Mortgage Business and Chief
Administrative Officer

Gordon Smith
Co-CEO of Consumer and Community Banking

Louis Rauchenberger
Head of Treasury and Security Services

Lee R. Raymond
Director
*Other affiliations: Retired Chairman and CEO, Exxon
Mobil*

David C. Novak
Director
Retired 2012

James S. Crown
Director

Laban P. Jackson, Jr.
Director
Other affiliations: Bank One Corporation

William C. Weldon
Director

Stephen B. Burke
Director
*Other affiliations: President, CEO, and Director at
NBCUniversal Media LLC.*

David M. Cote
Director

Crandall Close Bowles
Director

Ellen V. Futter
Director

William H. Gray III
Director
Retired 2012

Gaby Abdelnour
CEO of Asia Pacific
Retired 2012

Mary Callahan Erdoes
CEO of Asset Management

Samuel Todd Maclin
Co-CEO of Consumer and Business Banking and
Member of Operating Committee

Matthew E. Zames
Chief Investment Officer

Jimmy Lee
Vice Chairman

Richard M. Cashin
Executive of Private Equity
Other affiliations: New York City Investment Fund, Inc.

Catherine M. Keating
CEO of Americas Institutional Asset Management

Stephanie B. Mudick
Executive Vice President, Office of Consumer Practices

Morgan Stanley
1585 Broadway
New York, New York 10036
United States of America

The following people hold management positions
at Morgan Stanley and can be reached at Morgan
Stanley's corporate address, above.

James P. Gorman
Chief Executive Officer and President
Other affiliations: Visa USA, Inc.

Thomas Colm Kelleher
Chief Financial Officer

Walid A. Chammah
Co-President

Gregory J. Fleming
Head of Asset Management and Research

Paul J. Taubman
Co-Head of Institutional Securities

Francis P. Barron
Chief Legal Officer
Retired 2012

Ruth Porat
Chief Financial Officer, Executive Vice President

Charles D. Johnston
Head of Morgan Stanley Smith Barney
Other affiliations: Citigroup, Inc.; Smith Barney Inc.

Kenneth Michael deRegt
Chief Risk Officer

Paul C. Wirth
Finance Director/Controller

Keishi Hotsuki
Chief Risk Officer

Jim Rosenthal
Chief Operating Officer

Erskine B. Bowles
Director

James W. Owens
Director

Donald T. Nicolaisen
Director

Laura D. Tyson
Director

Roy J. Bostock
Director

Hutham S. Olayan
Director

Howard J. Davies
Director

C. Robert Kidder
Director
Other affiliations: Chrysler Group LLC.

John J. Mack
Senior Advisor

James H. Hance, Jr.
Former Director

Wells Fargo
420 Montgomery St.
San Francisco, CA 94163
United States of America

The following people hold management positions
at Wells Fargo and can be reached at Wells
Fargo's corporate address, above.

John G. Stumpf
Chief Executive Officer, Chairman of the Board,
Director, and President

David M. Carroll
Senior Executive Vice President of Wealth
Management, Brokerage, and Retirement Service
Operations

Julie M. White
Former Wells Fargo Executive and Vice President of
Human Resources

Mark C. Oman
Senior Executive Vice President 2005-2009

Michael J. Loughlin
Executive Vice President, Chief Risk Officer

James M. Strother
Senior Executive Vice President and General Counsel

Richard D. Levy
Executive Vice President and Controller

David A. Hoyt
Senior Executive Vice President and Head of the
Wholesale Banking Group

Avid Modjtabai
Executive Vice President Consumer Lending

Kevin A. Rhein
Executive Vice President Technology and Operations

Patricia R. Callahan
Senior Executive Vice President

Michael J. Heid
Executive Vice President and Member of the
Operating Committee
Other affiliations: Fannie Mae

Stephen W. Sanger
Director

Donald M. James
Director

John D. Baker II
Director

Enrique Hernandez, Jr.
Director

Philip J. Quigley
Director

Nicholas G. Moore
Independent Director

Susan E. Engel
Director

Cynthia H. Milligan
Director

Lloyd H. Dean
Director

John S. Chen
Director
Other affiliations: Walt Disney Co.

Susan G. Swenson
Director

Judith M. Runstad
Director

Elaine Chao
Director

Timothy J. Sloan
Chief Financial Officer

Selected Bank

Settlements

I N THE 1990S, CONGRESS "MODERNIZED" OUR banking system by undoing and eroding the laws—often
called "regulations"—that had been put in place after the
Great Depression to forestall another crash. In 2007–
2008, that new crash came.

After our government bailed out the banks with tax
money from the Treasury, returning the banks to business and quick profitability, many Americans had ques-
tions. Are our laws for banks strong enough? Had the
banks done anything wrong—anything illegal?

Since then we've seen some of what the banks
were doing between 2003 and 2008, as well as the new
and continuing violations the banks have committed
between 2008 and 2012. This proof has come from civil
and criminal complaints brought before court after
investigations by the Department of Justice, the Attorneys General of most of the fifty States, the Securities
and Exchange Commission, the Commodity Futures
Trading Commission, the Department of the Treasury, the IRS, the Federal Reserve Bank of New York,

the Office of the Comptroller of the Currency, and the Department of Housing and Urban Development.

Some allegations and evidence are revealed to the public when the banks accused of breaking the law reach a settlement. Guilt is generally not acknowledged by banks; they settle, often for large sums, in lieu of trial. The banks can easily afford these cash or promissory settlements, which spare them from more costly client lawsuits. Sometimes the banks don't even have to pay the government in the settlements, as long as they promise not to violate the same laws yet again.

A reader may wonder if the abuses described by individual letter-writers in *The Trouble is the Banks* have been documented elsewhere, or if they happened to anybody else. To answer in part, the following summaries offer a few highlights from four years of settlements.

– Eds.

Settlements Involving More Than One Bank

THE NATIONAL MORTGAGE CHARGES AND SETTLEMENT

A civil action filed several years after the housing crisis by the States Attorneys General and the US Government against five banks—Bank of America, Citi, Chase, GMAC/Ally Financial, and Wells Fargo—bundled the majority of consumer-level abuses and crimes that investigators had discovered into a single joint state-federal action, leading finally to a negotiated group settlement in which the banks agreed to pay a total of $29 billion to the states and various federal agencies, some of it intended to repay foreclosure victims.

It is extremely helpful to see the crimes and "wrongful practices" discovered in investigations by the 49 States Attorneys General, the US Justice Department, the Treasury, and the Department of Housing and Urban Development all in one place, constituting the charges that the five mortgage-lending banks agreed to pay so much money to be released from. (The one missing state, Oklahoma, arranged a separate settlement with the banks.) The state-federal government complaint in *United States v. Bank of America Corp.* (2012) specifies that one or more of the banks in question engaged in every one of the violations of law it details, but also that in many cases all five of the banks broke each law, engaging in the same patterns of "unfair, deceptive, and unlawful" practices. Here is what the government investigations found. Please note that much of this language closely tracks the wording of the Attorneys General and Department of Justice, even where it is not in quotation marks; page numbers refer to their filing with the Court.

> In originating mortgages, the banks used "unfair and deceptive" practices that "caused borrowers... to enter into unaffordable mortgage loans that led to increased foreclosures" (28). In servicing mortgages for borrowers, they failed to apply payments to accounts, applied them late, and gave inaccurate account statements. They charged excessive or improper fees for defaults. They didn't watch over the third parties they hired to do mortgage servicing work. They imposed unnecessary insurance on borrowers, including those who were already adequately insured. They lied in response to consumer complaints. They neither kept nor trained the staff necessary to do the required mortgage servicing work (22).
>
> Despite having been awarded authority by the Federal Housing Authority to underwrite loans and attain government insurance to back those loans just on the banks' say-so (these specially trusted banks were called "Direct Endorsement Lenders"), the banks for their own enrichment knowingly failed to comply with these underwriting rules. They ignored required criteria of applicants' credit-worthiness, and failed to follow standards of quality control, causing hundreds of millions of dollars in taxpayer payments for insurance claims for these bad mortgages and loans to unqualified

borrowers, with more claims still likely to
come. The action singled out Bank of America
and Countrywide for special blame (29-33).

When conducting or managing foreclosures,
the banks violated federal foreclosure
requirements, failed to properly identify
who was foreclosing, charged improper fees,
created and presented false documents of
all kinds, prepared and filed affidavits
without personal knowledge of what they
asserted and without bothering to check or
verify if they were true. ("The practice of
repeated false attestation of information
is popularly known as 'robosigning.'") Banks
also knew that third parties they worked
with were robosigning on their behalf. They
filed affidavits in foreclosure proceedings
without properly notarizing them to meet
state laws. They faked the "identity,
office, or legal status" of their employees
filing documents in foreclosures, charged
a range of wrongful expenses, costs, and
fees for many parts of the process, and
kept simultaneous foreclosure and loan
modification processes going for borrowers,
deceiving them about the foreclosures (27-
28).

As parties to bankruptcy proceedings seeking
to recover money as creditors, the banks
filed pleadings and documents without
reasonable inquiries to check if they were
true and failed to supervise the attorneys,
contractors, and agents working for them. In
this way, they lied to the courts and made
false claims, failed to document claims,

and violated a variety of federal, state,
and local laws and court rules. The banks
"sought payment from debtors or bankruptcy
estates for amounts that the Banks were not
legally entitled to collect," including debts
that were never incurred, were larger than
what had been contracted, or that ignored
already agreed-upon loan modifications (35).
They filed claims without itemizations of
the principal, interest, and fees. They
faked or failed to document ownership of
their claims. They started "collection
activities against the debtor" without
being authorized by the court. They claimed
money on debts that had already been paid
or satisfied. They charged attorneys' fees
for documents they then withdrew or courts
rejected. Banks failed to apply payments,
letting them make wrongful claims of
default; they lied about who had signed
documents, to pretend personal knowledge;
they lied about notarization that hadn't
been done; didn't tell debtors, trustees,
and courts about changes they were making to
interest and charges; and failed to update
records even when bankruptcy proceedings
were dismissed or closed. They did all of
the above despite being told that these
"errors" were occurring and would continue
to occur unless they fixed their procedures
(34-38).

Even after receiving funds and US government
"monetary incentives" and stimulus in 2008,
specifically for loan modification and loss
mitigation (including through the "Making
Home Affordable" mortgage-relief program,

tied to the bailout of the banks), the banks
broke the requirements of the programs,
broke their contractual obligations, and
violated federal laws. They didn't do the
loan modification underwriting they'd said
they would, failed to gather the right
paperwork, understaffed modification
programs, inadequately trained what staff
there was, didn't establish processes to
modify loans, kept borrowers in "trial
modifications" for excessive lengths of
time, and wrongfully denied modification
applications. They failed to respond to
consumer inquiries, lied to consumers when
referring loans to foreclosure, and secretly
initiated foreclosures while the borrower
was "in good faith actively pursuing a loss
mitigation alternative" that they themselves
had offered. They lied to consumers while
selling off their houses in the middle
of modification and trial periods. They
misled them about how loss mitigation
would save consumers from foreclosure.
They falsely advised people they had to be
sixty days delinquent in payments before
they could qualify for a loan modification.
They miscalculated eligibility for loan
modifications and denied relief to eligible
borrowers. They said they'd process
applications promptly while delaying them.
They failed to process loan modification
applications they received. They gave "false
or deceptive reasons" for why they denied
applications (19-26).

See: United States of America et al v. Bank of America
Corporation, (D.D.C. 2012)(No. 1:12-CV-00361).

MUNICIPAL BOND REINVESTMENT BID-RIGGING

JP Morgan Securities, Wells Fargo, GE Capital, UBS Financial Services, and Banc of America Securities have agreed to pay hundreds of millions of dollars to settle charges brought by the SEC, IRS, Department of Justice, Federal Reserve, Office of the Comptroller of the Currency, and a collection of States Attorneys General that they engaged in a massive interbank conspiracy to fix prices in the lucrative municipal bond reinvestment market, worth $3.7 trillion annually. When tax-exempt entities—including state and local governments, school districts, libraries, and hospitals—float a public bond issue to finance a capital project (the construction of a new school, for example), they get a large lump sum up front, even though they might not need to spend the cash for several years. IRS regulations require that the municipality invest that money at fair market value in the interim. The return on capital from that reinvestment can help defray the cost of borrowing, reducing costs to the taxpayers, who are ultimately responsible for repaying the municipality's bonds. To determine "fair market value," municipalities hire bidding agents to solicit "competitive" bids from large banks to reinvest the money on the municipality's behalf; the bank offering the highest return wins the business.

From at least 1997 through 2005, the banks operated as a cartel, directly stealing billions of dollars from taxpayers in all fifty states by reducing the rate of return that municipalities received on their reinvested capital.

Working alongside their supposed competitors and the bidding agents—who were hired to represent the municipal borrower's interests but received kickbacks from participating banks—traders on the banks' municipal derivatives desks would participate in three forms of bid rigging. Sometimes bidding agents would give traders "last looks," or inside information, on the highest competing bid so they could reduce their own to the bare minimum necessary to win the business. In other auctions, the bidding agents and banks would decide ahead of time which traders would win the auction, soliciting under-priced "set up" bids from other banks to depress the rate of return the winning bank would have to pay the municipality. Each bank both received "set ups" from other members of the group and submitted unreasonably low "set up" bids when it was another bank's turn to win some business. In addition to the settlements agreed to by the banks, at least eighteen traders and bank executives have been convicted of criminal conspiracy for their roles in the bid rigging scheme.

BANK, SETTLEMENT AMOUNT, AND DATE

JP Morgan Securities: $211 million (Jul. 7, 2011)

Wachovia (Wells Fargo): $148 million (Dec. 8, 2011)

GE Funding Capital Market Services: $70 million (Dec. 23, 2011)

UBS Financial Services: $160 million (May 4, 2011)

Banc of America Securities: $137 million (Dec. 7, 2010)

See: "SEC Charges Wachovia with Fraudulent Bond Rigging in Municipal Bonds Proceeds," SEC Press Release. Washington, DC, December 8, 2011; Reuters, "3 Ex-UBS Bankers Found Guilty of Rigging Bids," New York Times, August 31, 2012; Eric Dash, "JP Morgan Settles Bid-Rigging Case for $211 Million," New York Times, July 7, 2011; Complaint at SEC v. J.P. Morgan Securities LLC, (D.N.J. 2011) (No. 2:11-CV-03877).

EXCESSIVE OVERDRAFT FEES

In a series of class action lawsuits, Bank of America, JP Morgan Chase Bank, Wells Fargo Bank, and other major banks agreed to pay hundreds of millions of dollars to settle charges that they saddled checking account holders with unfair and excessive fees for "overdraft protection." As debit card transactions replaced paper checks as the most common way that consumers access money in their checking accounts, overdraft fees—assessed on customers making debit card transactions without enough money in the bank to pay for them—grew to constitute 74% of the fees banks earn from deposit accounts. Rather than simply rejecting debit transactions at the point of sale, the banks routinely charged account holders $35 fees to process even small payments that resulted in a negative balance. According to a 2008 FDIC analysis, overdraft fees such as these can carry an effective annualized interest rate of more than 3,500%. Moreover, the banks employed overdraft policies intended to maximize overdraft fee revenue at the expense of clarity and fairness toward some of their poorest customers: a study cited in the plaintiffs' civil complaint claims that 90% of overdraft fees are paid by the poorest 10% of a bank's customer base. For example, Bank of America would reorder debit card transactions in processing, posting the largest expenditures first, so that a series of small transactions would trigger the most possible overdraft fees even when there were sufficient funds in the account at the time of some purchases. As a matter of policy, the banks did not allow customers to opt out of their overdraft "protection" programs, didn't alert customers before approving transactions that would result in overdraft fees, and delayed posting large transactions to increase the number of charges on which it could later charge fees.

BANK, SETTLEMENT AMOUNT, AND DATE

Bank of America: $410 million (Nov. 22, 2011)

Wells Fargo Bank: $203 million (Aug. 11, 2010)

RBS–Citizens Bank: $137.5 million (Apr. 25, 2012)

JP Morgan Chase Bank: $110 million (May 25, 2012)

PNC Bank: $90 million (Jun. 26, 2012)

TD Bank: $62 million (May 11, 2012)

US Bancorp: $55 million (Jul. 2, 2012)

See: Andrew Martin, "Bank of America to Settle Over-
drafts Suit for \$410 Million," <u>New York Times</u>, May 23,
2011; Complaint at Ralph Tornes v. Bank of America, N.A.,
(No. 08-23323-CIV)(S.D. FL. 2010); "Wells Fargo Overdraft
Lawsuit: Bank Ordered to Pay \$203 Million in Fees Over
'Unfair' Charges," <u>Huffington Post</u>, August 8, 2010; Halah
Touryalai, "Shady Overdraft Fees Could Cost Banks Over \$1
Billion," <u>Forbes</u>, July 2, 2012; Jonathan Stempel and Nate
Raymond, "RBS Citizens Settles Overdraft-Fees Case for
\$137.5 Million," <u>Reuters</u>, April 25, 2012; David Voreacos
and Susannah Nesmith, "TD Bank Agrees to Pay \$62 Million in
Overdraft Fee Lawsuit," May 11, 2012; Reuters, "Court OKs
\$110M JP Morgan Overdraft Settlement," <u>Chicago Tribune</u>, May
25, 2012.

AUCTION RATE SECURITIES

In late 2008 and 2009, a list of major banks agreed to
settlements worth tens of billions of dollars to resolve
charges by the SEC, the New York Attorney General, and
other government agencies that they lied to investors
about the liquidity of investments into which billions of
dollars had flowed. Auction Rate Securities (ARS) are a
type of debt instrument that allows borrowers to float
corporate, student loan, or municipal debt with a vari-
able short-term interest rate, which is reset every seven
to thirty five days by a process called a "dutch auction."
Issuers benefit from short-term financing rates that are
generally lower than long-term rates charged for bank
loans. Introduced in the 1980s, ARS were marketed by
banks as highly liquid, "cash equivalent" investments;

in many cases, banks marketed the securities under misleading names such as "commercial paper" or "28-day liquid paper." However, this liquidity is entirely dependent on immediate credit conditions each time the ARS roll over through a new auction. Indeed, many of the banks' salespeople were insufficiently educated about the technical aspects of ARS, and banks took no action to correct this, even though they knew retail investors were not receiving proper explanations of the risks intrinsic to the ARS model. By early 2008, the ARS market grew to approximately $300 billion.

In general, the banks issuing the securities would act as market makers, submitting auction bids when none were forthcoming from investors in order to maintain liquidity and prevent the auctions from failing. However, as credit markets tightened in late 2007 and early 2008, the issuing banks were amassing larger inventories of ARS, as declining investor demand required them to step in more frequently to prevent failed auctions. In the fall of 2007, as bank executives grew concerned about their institutions' massive exposure to the increasingly illiquid ARS (particularly notes linked to student loans), pressure grew within the bank to sell off their inventories. The banks continued to sell their ARS stockpiles as safe, liquid investments—even though they were sounding internal alarms that conditions had deteriorated to the point where the auctions would fail outright without the banks' support. By February 2008, the banks' own balance sheets had been stretched thin under the weight of their exposure to the subprime mortgage market (among other troublesome asset classes), and one by one, the banks began allowing the roll-over auctions to fail. Once failure spread, internal alerts within the banks warned that retail investors who thought they had purchased "cash alternatives" could instead be stuck holding the notes for thirty years or longer, unable to liquidate their positions. In fact, investors could no longer access the billions of dollars of capital collectively tied up in their ARS. They were unable to use that money on demand, as promised, to satisfy other obligations, such as their own mortgage, student loan, or credit card payments. Without admitting guilt, the banks settled with the government, agreeing to pay hundreds of millions in fines, and to repurchase about $61 billion worth of ARS from investors at par or compensate those who had been forced to sell their holdings at crushing discounts.

BANK, SETTLEMENT AMOUNT, AND DATE

UBS Securities: $22.7 billion (Aug. 8, 2008)

Citigroup Global Markets: $7 billion (Aug. 7, 2008)

Merrill Lynch: $7 billion (August 22, 2008)

Wachovia Securities (Wells Fargo): $7 billion (Feb. 5, 2009)

Banc of America Securities: $4.5 billion (Jun. 3, 2009)

Morgan Stanley: $4.5 billion (Aug. 14, 2008)

JP Morgan Chase: $3 billion (Aug. 14, 2008)

Deutsche Bank: $1.3 billion (Jun. 3, 2009)

Selected Bank Settlements

Goldman Sachs: $1 billion (Aug. 21, 2008)

RBC: $800 million (Jun. 3, 2009)

TD Ameritrade: $456 million (Jul. 20, 2009)

See: "SEC Finalizes ARS Settlements with Citigroup and UBS, Providing Nearly $30 Billion in Liquidity to Investors," SEC Press Release. Washington, D.C., December 11, 2008; "SEC Finalizes Settlements with Bank of America, RBC, and Deutsche Bank," SEC Press Release. Washington, D.C., June 3, 2009; "Goldman Sachs Settles with State Regulators and Offers to Repurchase Auction Rate Securities Sold to its Private Clients," Goldman Sachs Press Release. New York, August 21, 2008; Complaint at SEC v. Banc of America Securities LLC (S.D.N.Y. 2009) (No. 09-cv-5170); "SEC Enforcement Division Announces Preliminary Settlement with Merrill Lynch to Help Auction Rate Security Investors," SEC Press Release. Washington D.C., August 22, 2008; "SEC Finalizes ARS Settlement to Provide $7 Billion in Liquidity to Wachovia Investors," SEC Press Release. Washington D.C., February 5, 2009.

Settlements by Bank

BANK OF AMERICA
Owns Merrill Lynch and Countrywide Mortgage

ON SEPTEMBER 13, 2012, Bank of America reached a settlement with the Department of Justice and the US Department of Housing and Urban Development, agreeing to pay up to $5,000 to mortgage applicants who were improperly asked for doctors' letters describing the disabilities that qualified them for Social Security Disability Insurance (SSDI). As part of the settlement, Bank of America will hire a third-party administrator to review 25,000 mortgage applications and identify cases in which the bank's requests for information violated the Fair Housing Act and the Equal Credit Opportunity Act. The mortgage applications of many victims in this case were denied after they refused to comply with invasive demands for detailed medical information about the nature and severity of their disabilities—requests which applicants rightly suspected constituted illegal discrimination on the basis of handicap and the receipt of public assistance. In the settlement, Bank of America denied the allegations that its policies constituted discrimination.

See: Danielle Douglas, "Bank of America Settles Loan Discrimination Charges," Washington Post, September 14, 2012; Complaint at United States v. Bank of America N.A., D/B/A Bank of America, Home Loans, (W.D.N.C. 2012) (No. 3:12-CV-00605).

ON FEBRUARY 9, 2012, Bank of America agreed to pay
$1 billion to settle charges—brought by the Depart-
ment of Justice, the Inspectors General of the Troubled
Asset Relief Program, and the Federal Housing Finance
Agency—that the Countrywide Financial Corporation,
which the bank acquired for $4.5 billion during the
financial crisis, perpetrated a massive mortgage fraud.
The investigation revealed that Countrywide defrauded
the government by originating and underwriting tens of
thousands of government-insured mortgages based on
inflated appraisals. Countrywide also sold mortgages to
borrowers that it knew were unqualified for the loans.
These mortgages were insured by the Federal Housing
Administration through a program meant to provide
assistance to low-income and first-time home buyers.
When these borrowers defaulted en masse, the Federal Housing Administration had to pay hundreds of
millions of dollars in insurance claims and left people
across the country with debts greater than the value of
their homes. Half of the settlement—which constituted
the largest penalty ever assessed under the False Claims
Act—was paid directly to the FHA, while the remaining $500 million were allocated to a loan modification
program for mortgage borrowers who found themselves
underwater as their artificially inflated home values
plummeted.

See: Robert Nadoza, "$1 Billion to Be Paid by The Bank Of
America to The United States. Largest False Claims Act
Settlement Relating to Mortgage Fraud," Eastern Dis-
trict of New York United States Attorney's Office Press
Release. February 9, 2012; Nelson D. Schwartz and Shaila

The Trouble is the Banks

Dewan, "States Negotiate $26 Billion Agreement for Home-owners," <u>New York Times</u>, February 8, 2012.

ON DECEMBER 21, 2011, Bank of America agreed to pay $335 million to settle charges brought by the Department of Justice over the Countrywide Financial Corporation's predatory lending practices. From 2004 to 2008—the time period covering Countrywide's booming subprime lending spree, its collapse, and its purchase by Bank of America—its loan officers and mortgage brokers systematically steered more than 200,000 qualified African American and Latino borrowers into unnecessarily expensive and burdensome subprime loans when similarly qualified white borrowers were sold less expensive prime loans. Countrywide permitted its employees to vary the fees, terms, and interest rates it offered to borrowers for reasons unrelated to objective creditworthiness, despite knowing that this discretion was being used to discriminate on the basis of race and national origin. These borrowers were then saddled with subprime loan obligations that had higher interest rates and more punitive fees than the prime loans they qualified for under Countrywide's own underwriting standards.

The settlement also resolves charges that Countrywide violated the Equal Opportunity Credit Act by encouraging non-applicant spouses of mortgage borrowers to sign documents that transferred all their legal rights and economic interests in jointly-held property to their borrowing spouses. The $335 million turned over by Bank of America went to compensating victims of Countrywide's predatory lending practices.

Selected Bank Settlements

See: Charlie Savage, "Countrywide Will Settle a Bias
Suit," New York Times, December 21, 2011; "Justice
Department Reaches $335 Million Settlement to Resolve
Allegations of Lending Discrimination by Countrywide
Financial Corporation," Department of Justice Press
Release. December 21, 2011.

ON MAY 26, 2011, Bank of America agreed to pay $20 million to settle charges, brought by the Department of Justice under the Servicemembers Civil Relief Act, that Countrywide Home Loans Servicing wrongfully foreclosed upon approximately 160 active duty servicemembers without obtaining required court orders. Beginning in at least 2006, Countrywide initiated foreclosure proceedings against borrowers without conducting necessary military status checks. The $20 million will go to compensating victims of illegal foreclosures. As part of its agreement, Countrywide agreed to train its employees to check borrowers' military status in Pentagon databases and in its own files before foreclosing on servicemembers.

See: "Justice Department Settles with Bank of America and
Saxon Mortgage for Illegally Foreclosing on Servicemembers," Department of Justice Press Release. May 26, 2011.

ON DECEMBER 31, 2010, Bank of America paid $2.8 billion to settle charges from the Federal Housing Finance Agency that the Countrywide Financial Corporation sold hundreds of billions of dollars worth of fraudulent mortgages to Fannie Mae and Freddie Mac. Fannie and Freddie collapsed in 2008 under the weight of failing loans, many of which had been sold under false pretenses. Because the terms of these sales (which obligated mortgage underwriters and originators to repurchase defaulting mortgages) were later revealed to have contained falsifications, industry analysts described the settlement as a "gift" to Bank of America: $2.8 billion was a small sum compared to the estimated $10 billion in liabilities the bank was facing. According to the terms of the settlement, the bank's $1.3 billion payment to Freddie Mac extinguishes all future claims and repurchase obligations on the approximately 787,000 mortgages at issue, which had an unpaid principal of $127 billion at the time of the agreement. The $1.5 billion settlement with Fannie Mae similarly absolves the bank of responsibility for 12,045 loans with an outstanding principal balance of $2.7 billion, but leaves open repurchase obligations on an additional 5,760 loans—a $1.3 billion liability. Since both Fannie and Freddie became wards of the state under the terms of their 2008 bailouts, taxpayers are ultimately responsible for any further losses they incur.

See: David S. Hilzenrath, "Bank of America Settles Mortgage Dispute with Fannie Mae, Freddie Mac," Washington Post, January 3, 2011.

ON OCTOBER 15, 2010, Angelo Mozilo, the disgraced former CEO of Countrywide Financial, agreed to pay $67.5 million to settle the SEC's civil fraud charges just days before the case was slated to go to trial. Mozilo, who collected an estimated $521.5 million in total compensation during the eight-year period before he left the company in 2008, is the most prominent executive of a financial company to be held personally liable for the actions leading to the financial crisis. The SEC not only charged Mozilo with lying to Countrywide's investors by hiding the abysmal quality of the subprime loans in the firm's portfolio, but also charged Mozilo with insider trading for unloading millions of dollars in stock in 2006 before the company's fatal problems had been made public. As part of the settlement, Mozilo agreed to a lifetime ban from holding any officer or director position in a public company. Thanks to an indemnification agreement, however, $20 million of the penalty levied against Mozilo was paid by Bank of America, which purchased Countrywide in January 2008.

See: "Former Countrywide CEO Angelo Mozilo to Pay SEC's Largest-Ever Financial Penalty Against a Public Company's Senior Executive," SEC Enforcement Division Press Release. October 15, 2010; Gretchen Morgenson, "Lending Magnate Settles Fraud Case," New York Times, October 15, 2010.

ON JUNE 7, 2010, two Bank of America loan servicing subsidiaries, Countrywide Home Loans and BAC Home Loans Servicing, agreed to pay $108 million to settle charges brought by the Federal Trade Commission that it overcharged homeowners facing foreclosure with inflated and hidden fees, while simultaneously making false or unsupported claims to borrowers about the amount of their debts. Loan servicing companies routinely charge defaulting borrowers for services that protect the lenders' interests in properties awaiting foreclosure and add these charges onto borrowers' outstanding balances. According to the FTC's complaint, when borrowers fell behind on payments, Countrywide frequently ordered unnecessary services—such as property inspections and lawn mowing—for which they charged borrowers as much as $300. To boost profits from fees, Countrywide created subsidiaries to hire the contractors actually doing the work rather than hiring these vendors directly—a strategy that allowed Countrywide to mark up the prices charged by the vendors doing the work by as much as 100%. Countrywide would attempt to recover these fees by foreclosure, pursuing borrowers aggressively after they left the protection of bankruptcy court. According to the settlement documents filed with the court, the money recovered will go to reimburse overcharged homeowners, but the companies did not admit the allegations.

See: Federal Trade Commission v. Countrywide Home Loans, Inc., and BAC Home Loans Servicing, LP, (C.D. Cal. 2010) (No. CV-10-4193); Edward Wyatt, "Countrywide Settles Fee Dispute," New York Times, June 7, 2010.

IN THE SUMMER OF 2010, Bank of America agreed to pay a total of $9.1 billion to settle a pair of lawsuits brought forward by investors who suffered damages due to Countrywide Financial's fraudulent mortgage practices during the housing boom. In the larger of the two settlements, the bank paid $8.5 billion to investors who lost money when mortgage bonds they purchased from Countrywide failed. The bonds were backed by the poor-quality mortgages Countrywide sold during the boom. In the second settlement, the bank agreed to pay $600 million to settle a class-action lawsuit in which Countrywide's investors accused the company of concealing mounting risks on its balance sheet when, in its rush to sell subprime mortgages, it loosened mortgage-underwriting standards. The suit, led by New York State and City pension funds, also named as defendants several Countrywide executives and the financial firms that underwrote its stock, though the settlement terms clear them of liability.

See: Associated Press, "$600 Million Countrywide Settlement," New York Times, August 3, 2012; Wall Street Journal, "BoA Haunted by Countrywide Deal," June 30, 2011.

CHASE
AKA JP Morgan Chase. Owns Bear Stearns, EMC Mortgage, Washington Mutual Bank

ON JUNE 6, 2012, JP Morgan Chase & Co. agreed to pay $150 million to three union pension funds representing investors whose retirement savings were lost when the bank placed their money in an investment vehicle that collapsed in the financial crisis. These three funds were the AFTRA Retirement Fund, the Imperial County Employees' Retirement System, and the Investment Committee of the Manhattan and Bronx Surface Transit Operating System. The suit charged that JP Morgan had breached its fiduciary duties of "prudence" and "loyalty" by placing the funds' capital in medium-term notes issued by Sigma Finance Corp, a structured investment vehicle that collapsed in 2008. The plaintiffs allege that while JP Morgan invested $500 million of the retirement funds' money in the Sigma notes, another part of the bank was extending billions of dollars in emergency "repo" financing to the unstable investment vehicle. Despite knowing about these signs of fiscal distress and the retirement funds' deteriorating legal position, the JP Morgan desk controlling their capital maintained their investment in the Sigma notes. When Sigma collapsed in September 2008, JP Morgan made collateral calls on its repo loans and an appointed receiver auctioned off Sigma's remaining assets. While the retirement funds received about six cents on the dollar, JP Morgan made a $1.9 billion profit from its repo financing transaction.

See: Bon Van Voris, "JP Morgan's $150 Million Securities Lending Accord Approved," <u>Bloomberg</u>, June 6, 2012; Complaint at <u>Board of Trustees of the AFTRA Retirement Fund v. JP Morgan Chase Bank N.A.,</u> (S.D.N.Y. 2011) (No. 09-CV-00686).

ON APRIL 4, 2012, JP Morgan Chase Bank agreed to pay a $20 million fine to settle charges brought by the CFTC that in its banking relationship with the now-defunct Lehman Brothers Inc., it failed to properly segregate the firm's customers' funds from the firm's proprietary capital. JP Morgan served as a depository institution for Lehman, holding deposits of the firm's customers' funds that varied in size, but almost always totaled over $250 million at a time. Simultaneously, the bank provided Lehman with an intra-day line of credit to facilitate its proprietary trading activities. The amount of intra-day credit that JP Morgan would extend to Lehman depended on the firm's "net free equity" held at the bank. Starting on November 17, 2006 and continuing until Lehman's 2008 collapse, JP Morgan included the customers' funds held on deposit in its calculation of Lehman's net free equity, even though that money did not belong to the firm but to its customers. The Commodity Exchange Act not only prohibits depository institutions from treating customer funds as belonging to anyone other than those customers, but also bans them from using customer funds as a basis on which to extend credit to anyone but those customers. JP Morgan violated these fundamental rules, and also refused to return Lehman's customers' funds when requested on September 15, 2008, as the firm's collapse picked up speed, citing the fund's negative free equity. This situation continued for two weeks, until the bank responded to a CFTC order to release the customer funds.

In a separate settlement, JP Morgan agreed to pay $861 million in cash and securities to customers of Lehman Brothers' collapsed broker-dealer business. JP Morgan was the primary clearing agent for Lehman Brothers. The investors' claims stem from JP Morgan's failure to liquidate holdings of securities it maintained following Lehman's 2008 failure.

See: Ben Protess and Azam Ahmed, "Regulators Penalize JP Morgan Over Lehman Ties," <u>New York Times</u>, April 4, 2012; "CFTC Orders JP Morgan Chase Bank, N.A. to Pay a $20 Million Civil Monetary Penalty to Settle CFTC Charges of Unlawfully Handling Customer Segregated Funds." U.S. Commodity Futures Trading Commission Press Release, April 4, 2012; Joseph Checkler, "Judge Clears $861 Million J.P. Morgan-Lehman Settlement," <u>Wall Street Journal</u>, June 23, 2011.

ON JUNE 21, 2011, JP Morgan Securities agreed to pay $153.6 million to settle the SEC's charges that it lied to investors, selling them pieces of a $1.1 billion collateralized debt obligation (CDO) without disclosing that the subprime mortgage securities packaged within it were selected by an outside hedge fund that had a $600 million bet against those same securities. In the marketing materials for its "Squared CDO 2007-1," JP Morgan

Securities touted the "fact" that it had employed GSC Capital Corp, a firm experienced in monitoring CDO credit risk, to select promising assets that the bank would package into Squared CDO 2007-1. However, an SEC investigation revealed that a hedge fund operated by Magnetar Capital LLC played a secret but significant role in the selection of assets, picking securities on which it had already amassed a $600 million short position using credit default swaps. Although JP Morgan Securities was aware that Magnetar's economic interest was diametrically opposed to Squared CDO 2007-1's investors—pension funds, retirement funds, and insurance companies—the bank failed to disclose the hedge fund's role in constructing the CDO, meanwhile mounting an aggressive global effort to sell a CDO that had been designed to fail. When the CDO defaulted after less than a year, investors lost the hundreds of millions of dollars they had invested, and Magnetar cashed in on its short position. In the settlement agreement, JP Morgan Securities neither admits nor denies the SEC's charges.

In the same settlement, JP Morgan Securities announced it would voluntarily pay $56.7 million back to investors in a similar transaction, "Tahoma CDO I," which failed. The SEC did not bring any action related to the Tahoma deal.

See: Edward Wyatt, "JP Morgan Settles Case With S.E.C.," New York Times, June 21, 2011; Complaint at SEC v. J.P. Morgan Securities LLC (f/k/a J.P. Morgan Securities Inc.), (S.D.N.Y. 2011) (No. 11-CV-131).

The Trouble is the Banks

ON DECEMBER 22, 2010, JP Morgan Chase agreed to pay the state of Florida $25 million to settle charges from the Florida Attorney General that it sold unregistered securities to a state-run money market fund, called the Local Government Investment Pool. JP Morgan sold the unregistered securities to the fund, violating the SEC registration requirement of the Securities Act of 1933. After the asset-backed securities defaulted, the public fund experienced a run on deposits. The fund, which had assets of $27 billion in November 2007, had only $6.9 billion left at the time of the settlement. In its settlement, JP Morgan "neither admits nor denies" the allegations.

See: Jerry Hart, "JP Morgan Agrees to Pay Florida $25 Million for Bond Sales to Muni Fund," Bloomberg, December 22, 2010.

CITI

AKA Citigroup. Owner of Citibank, CitiMortgage

ON FEBRUARY 15, 2012, CitiMortgage agreed to pay $158 million to settle charges brought by the US Attorney for the Southern District of New York that it fed tens of thousands of mortgage loans into a Federal Housing Administration program that insures banks against the costs incurred when borrowers default. In the settlement, CitiMortgage "admits, acknowledges, and accepts responsibility" for undermining its own quality-control teams, which certify that loans submitted to the FHA are free from fraud and other "defects" that would prohibit a government guarantee. With the quality-control teams under pressure from the lenders (described in court documents as "brute force"), the company endorsed nearly 30,000 mortgages with required certifications that were "knowingly or recklessly false" since 2004. CitiMortgage's failure to conduct basic due diligence and its regular practice of submitting loans to the guarantee program that clearly violated the FHA's underwriting standards led to more than 30% of those mortgages ending up in default—including 47% of those sold in 2006 and 2007—costing the federal government millions of dollars in insurance payouts and triggering thousands of foreclosures.

See: Associated Press, "Citigroup to Pay $158 Million in Mortgage Settlement," <u>New York Times</u>, February 15, 2012; "Manhattan U.S. Attorney Files and Simultaneously Settles Fraud Lawsuit Against Citimortgage, Inc. for Reckless Mortgage Lending Practices," Southern District of New

The Trouble is the Banks

York U.S. Attorney's Office Press Release. February 15, 2012.

ON OCTOBER 19, 2011, Citigroup agreed to pay $285 million to settle the SEC's charges that it defrauded investors when its broker-dealer subsidiary sold them a $1 billion mortgage-backed "CDO-squared"—a CDO backed by tranches of other CDOs—without disclosing that it had designed the investment to fail. Citibank's marketing documents claimed that the particular assets packaged into the highly leveraged CDO, named "Class V Funding III," were selected by an independent "collateral manager," Credit Suisse Alternative Capital—an arrangement intended to ensure that only securities likely to perform well would be included. In reality, Credit Suisse permitted Citigroup to pick half, or $500 million worth, of Class V Funding III's assets. Rather than selecting these securities for their strength, Citigroup had picked this list because one of its proprietary trading desks wished to "short" them with a $500 million bet that they would rapidly decline in value. When Class V Funding III was declared to be in default in November 2007, less than nine months after the deal closed, its fifteen investors lost everything. Citigroup earned $34 million in fees for structuring the CDO and made a $126 million net profit on its secret short position.

As is the norm in the SEC's settlements, Citigroup agreed to cut a check while neither admitting nor denying the SEC's allegations, an arrangement that protects the bank from exposure to investors' civil suits, which could otherwise use the government's findings as evidence. However, the Federal District Judge presiding over this case, Jed S. Rakoff, rejected the settlement's generous terms, writing that the proposal was "neither fair, nor reasonable, nor adequate, nor in the public interest." Further, in a direct rejection of the SEC's usual practice, he argued that by allowing the bank to avoid acknowledgement of its findings, the agency had denied him an evidentiary basis on which to evaluate the settlement's justification. The opinion is as notable for its criticism of the SEC's willingness to deprive the public "of ever knowing the truth in a matter of obvious public importance" as it is for its condemnation of Citigroup, which Judge Rakoff accurately labels "a recidivist." Unfortunately, following Judge Rakoff's celebrated November 2011 opinion, the case veered back toward the path usually followed by SEC investigations: In March 2012, the Federal Court of Appeals ruled that there is a "strong likelihood" that Judge Rakoff erred in his opinion, writing that "requiring such an admission would in most cases undermine any chance for compromise." And finally, in August 2012, a federal jury acquitted Brian Stoker, the midlevel Citigroup executive directly responsible for Class V Funding III, of charges brought by the SEC. The jury's verdict was accompanied by an unusual statement, read aloud in court by Judge Rakoff, that encouraged the Commission to continue bringing cases against large banks and their high-level executives.

See: Complaint at <u>SEC v. Citigroup Global Markets Inc.</u>, (S.D.N.Y. 2011) (No. 11-CV-7387); Edward Wyatt, "Judge Blocks Citigroup Settlement with S.E.C.," <u>New York Times</u>, November 28, 2011; Peter Lattman, "S.E.C Gets

The Trouble is the Banks

Encouragement from Jury that Ruled Against It," <u>New York Times</u>, August 3, 2012.

ON JULY 29, 2010, Citigroup and two former executives paid approximately $75 million in penalties to settle the SEC's charges that the financial services conglomerate repeatedly lied to investors about its investment banking unit's holdings of assets backed by subprime mortgages. In both conference calls with investors and on regulatory filings submitted to the SEC during the height of the 2007 financial panic, Citigroup's CFO and head of investor relations stated that the bank had reduced its exposure to subprime mortgage-backed assets to $13 billion. However, this figure failed to include more than $40 billion in additional exposure to that troublesome sector in the form of highly rated pieces of subprime CDOs and contracts, called "liquidity puts," that obligated the bank to repurchase illiquid CDOs back from buyers if no one else would. Internal Citigroup documents show that the executives used the false $13 billion figure on calls and in SEC filings they drafted, even though they had been briefed multiple times on the bank's complete subprime portfolio and warned that the bank's disclosures were misleading investors about the additional $40 billion risk it carried on its books. In the settlement, Citigroup neither admitted nor denied the SEC's allegations.

ON AUGUST 30, 2012, Citigroup agreed to pay $590 million to settle a class action suit that accused the bank of making similar misrepresentations to investors about its subprime mortgage portfolio. The money will go to investors who purchased stock in the financial giant between February 2007 and April 2008; Citigroup's market value had dropped by over $110 billion during that period.

See: Complaint at <u>SEC v. Citigroup Inc.,</u> (D.D.C. 2010) (No. 1:10-CV-01277); "Citi to Settle Suit for $590 Million," <u>Wall Street Journal</u>, August 30, 2012.

WELLS FARGO
Owns Wachovia

ON JULY 12, 2012, Wells Fargo Bank agreed to pay $175 million to settle charges brought by the Department of Justice that it knowingly engaged in a pattern of discrimination against African American and Latino borrowers, charging them higher fees and steering them into more expensive subprime mortgages than similarly qualified white applicants. Wells Fargo, the largest home mortgage originator in the United States, improperly steered approximately 4,000 minority borrowers into high interest subprime loans even though their objective credit risk should have qualified them for prime loans with lower interest rates by the bank's own underwriting criteria. Between 2004 and 2008, Wells Fargo's African American applicants were 2.9 times more likely to end up in subprime loans than similar white borrowers; Latinos were 1.8 times more likely than whites to get worse loan terms. In addition, the bank overcharged 30,000 minority borrowers with discriminatory fees, charging African American applicants an average of $2,937 more than similar white borrowers for a $300,000 mortgage.

In settlement documents filed with the court, Wells Fargo denied that it ever discriminated on the basis of race or national origin.

See: Charlie Savage, "Wells Fargo Will Settle Mortgage Bias Charges," <u>New York Times</u>, July 7, 2012; Complaint at <u>United States of America v. Wells Fargo Bank, N.A.,</u> (D.D.C. 2012) (No. 1:12-CV-01150).

ON AUGUST 6, 2011, Wells Fargo agreed to pay $590 million to settle a class action lawsuit, led by a collection of public employee pension funds, alleging that Wachovia lied to investors about its exposure to tens of billions of dollars in losses related to its mortgage portfolio. The plaintiffs' civil complaint alleges that investors in a series of bonds and preferred securities offered between July 2006 and May 2008 were misled about the poor quality of adjustable rate– and subprime mortgages held by the bank. During that period, investors purchased about $35 billion in securities. Offering materials prepared by the bank and its accounting firm KPMG—which agreed to pay an additional $37 million dollars in the settlement—described the loan portfolio as having "pristine credit quality." In late 2008, Wachovia failed under the weight of its collapsed mortgaged portfolio and was purchased by Wells Fargo.

See: David Benoit Barouh, "Wells Fargo Agrees to Settle Wachovia Suit," <u>Wall Street Journal</u>, August 6, 2011.

ON JANUARY 8, 2010, Wells Fargo lost a tax-refund lawsuit against the US government, depriving the bank of $115 million in tax deductions it had engineered through a complex financing deal with municipal transit agencies. The so-called Sale-In-Lease-Out (SILO) deals allowed the bank to purchase the capital assets of twenty-six different entities—including rail cars from New Jersey Transit, train equipment from Washington DC's MARTA, and locomotives from Caltrans—and lease them back to the transit agencies. The "sea of paper and complexity" created by these deals allowed the bank to claim the unused tax deductions accrued by the depreciation of the capital assets. In rejecting the bank's claimed tax deductions, Judge Thomas Wheeler wrote that the SILO deals "lack economic substance and were intended only to reduce Wells Fargo's federal taxes." The judge was particularly critical of the involvement of well-known companies such as Ernst & Young and A.I.G., which was "window dressing serving only to generate fees and lengthy documents to give the SILOs an appearance of validity."

See: Erik Larsen, "Wells Fargo Loses $115 Million Tax-Deduction Lawsuit," <u>Bloomberg</u>, January 12, 2010.

GOLDMAN SACHS

ON APRIL 12, 2012, Goldman Sachs agreed to pay $22 million to settle charges by the SEC that during weekly "huddle" meetings, traders regularly shared material, nonpublic information about the firm's best short-term trading ideas and its accumulated "market color" with an exclusive group of high-volume clients. In 2007, Goldman formalized this exchange of insider information with its "Asymmetrical Service Initiative," under which research analysts called the firm's top clients following the traders' weekly "huddles" to share information and trading ideas. Goldman hoped that the program would improve the performance of the firm's traders and generate increased commissions from the selected clients.

See: Greg Chang, "Goldman Sachs to Pay $22 Million in Settlement with SEC, Finra," <u>Bloomberg</u>, April 12, 2012; "SEC Charges Goldman, Sachs & Co. Lacked Adequate Policies and Procedures for Research 'Huddles'," SEC Press Release. Washington, D.C., April 12, 2012.

ON JULY 15, 2010, Goldman, Sachs & Co. agreed to pay the SEC $550 million—at the time, the largest fine paid by a Wall Street bank—to settle charges that it misled investors about the construction and expected performance of a $2 billion CDO called ABACUS 2007-AC1. Although Goldman's marketing materials claimed that an independent firm called ACA Capital had selected the underlying mortgage-backed securities that were packaged into the ABACUS deal, Goldman never disclosed the hidden role played by the hedge fund Paulson

& Co. According to documents filed in federal court, Paulson, which was in the process of placing a multi-billion dollar bet against the collapsing sub-prime mortgage market, secretly paid Goldman Sachs $15 million to allow it to pack the ABACUS deal full of mortgage securities it predicted would fail. By January 2008, less than a year after the ABACUS deal closed, 99% of those underlying mortgage securities had failed, costing its investors over $1 billion and earning Paulson about $1 billion in profit. While Goldman paid the fine, the only individual named in the SEC suit was a 28-year-old midlevel trader named Fabrice "Fabulous Fab" Tourre, whose incriminating emails, sent to his girlfriend from his Goldman email account, earned him a civil fraud suit. In the settlement, Goldman Sachs neither admits nor denies the allegations.

See: Sewell Chan, "Goldman Pays $550 Million to Settle Fraud Case," New York Times, July 15, 2010; "Goldman Sachs to Pay Record $550 Million to Settle Charges Related to Subprime Mortgage CDO," SEC Press Release. Washington, D.C., July 15, 2010.

ON MAY 10, 2009, The Goldman Sachs Group agreed to pay up to $60 million to end an ongoing investigation by the Massachusetts Attorney General's office into the firm's mortgage servicing business, which the state argues promoted predatory lending practices. $50 million of the settlement went to fund a loan modification program, intended to reduce the principal on the outstanding mortgages of 714 Massachusetts residents, while the remainder went to the state. According to the

The Trouble is the Banks

Attorney General's office, Goldman's loan servicing company, Litton Loan Servicing LP, was aware that the mortgages it was buying up to feed Goldman's securitization efforts were originated using unfair and predatory practices.

See: Leslie Wayne, "Goldman Pays to End State Inquiry Into Loans," New York Times, May 11, 2009.